THE TRUE STORY

of the Allied Attack

on Dieppe in the Summer of 1942.

Desperate for a major Allied victory and assured of a good chance of success, the Allies committed thousands of Canadian, British, and American fighting men to the battle.

In the bitter land, sea, and air fight that followed, thousands of lives were lost on the French coast. The incredible losses at Dieppe crushed the hope for a decisive blow against the German coastal defense system, but the lessons learned were to make Allied victories possible.

We will send you a free catalog on request. Any titles not in your local book store can be purchased by mail. Send the price of the book plus 35¢ shipping charge to Belmont Tower Books, Two Park Avenue, New York, New York 10016.

Titles currently in print are available in quantity for industrial and sales promotion use at reduced rates. Address inquiries to our Promotion Department.

DIEPPE

HAROLD CALIN

BELMONT TOWER BOOKS ● NEW YORK CITY

A BELMONT TOWER BOOK

Published by

Tower Publications, Inc.
Two Park Avenue
New York, N.Y. 10016

Copyright © 1978 Tower Publications, Inc.

All rights reserved
Printed in the United States of America

Dieppe

1

Beneath the clear summer afternoon sky, the sunlight whitened the pale fields of Hampshire, as the convoy of military motor transports moved steadily along Route A3, intruding its heavy sounds across the tranquil English countryside. With seeming abruptness, the open fields were replaced by the low buildings of a village. The engines reverberated hollowly as the vehicles passed quickly through Petersfield, and townspeople standing beside the road waved to the uniformed men seated near the tailgates of the lorries. They had seen similar convoys pass along this route a short time before. The soldiers smiled and returned the waved greetings, looking back until a turn in the road obscured their line of sight. There was little traffic through the village, and shortly they were passing through open country again, moving south.

They came through Horndean, and some of the men, who had been on earlier training exercises in the Isle of Wight, recognized that they were on the road to Portsmouth and the Royal Naval dockyards.

They were a detachment of the Royal Regiment of Canada, and this transit was the opening phase of a movement exercise they had been told was code named "Ford I." But some five weeks before, they had been transported in a similar exercise, "Klondike I," and it had taken them, instead of to the Isle of Wight, onto infantry landing ships and three days of sealed quarters. They had been visited, in quarters, by the divisional commander, General Roberts, and by Vice Admiral Lord Louis Mountbatten, Chief of Combined Operations. There had been detailed briefings on an operation they were told would take place across the English Channel on the French coast at Dieppe.

And then the waiting had begun. It lasted three days, into the seventh of July, lying there aboard ship in the Yarmouth Roads near the west end of the Solent, and then four German bombers had attacked. A bomb hit the ship, but passed entirely through it before detonating. They had been landed, marched to another anchorage, and the waiting had begun again.

Five weeks ago, the waiting had ended through weather that worsened through two days more, until they were returned to the mainland and transported to their station in Surrey, south of London. The operation had been cancelled.

Now it was the afternoon of 18 August, 1942, and as the motor convoy passed on through Cosham, the men wondered if, indeed, they were being moved to yet another training exercise in the Isle of Wight. They continued south, through Portsmouth, and, as they expected, into the Royal Naval Yard. After a brief checkstop, the convoy moved through the yard, passing the drydocked H.M.S. Victory, the restored and preserved flagship on whose deck Nelson had been mortally wounded at the Battle of Trafalgar in 1805.

The lorries moved slowly now, passing over the rough cobbles, through the shadows of the huge cranes overhead, and then out onto a stone pierhead. The convoy stopped and the men were issued orders to detruck and assemble along the stone pavings of the pier.

The sun had moved visibly lower in the afternoon sky, deepening shadows and sharpening the sights across the naval yard, the movements of lorries and other vehicles across nearby pierheads. A column of troops filed slowly along the inclined ramp of a ship across a short stretch of water.

Berthed alongside the pierhead was a vessel that looked like a merchant ship. Hung from the davits along its main deck were the square, flat bottomed, snub nosed craft the men recognized from their training exercises as L.C.P.s (personnel landing craft), from which they had been put ashore to storm the empty beaches of the Isle of Wight in the training operations the month before. Under the rhythm of movements across the naval yard and the ringing metallic noises of operating machinery, there seemed an atmosphere of subdued silence.

As their column approached the boarding ramp of the ship, which they learned was the H.M.S. Queen Emma, they could see berthed nearby a sleek low hulled fighting ship. She was the "Hunt" class destroyer H.M.S. Calpe. There were groupings of men at the foot of the Calpe's boarding ramp, men in the uniforms of the Royal Navy as well as others they recognized as officers of their own Canadian regiment. There was much activity along the destroyer's decks, and a new sense of urgency infused itself through the troops as they made their way aboard the infantry landing ship, Queen Emma. Now they were suddenly out of the sunlight and filing through the dimly lit companionways below, joining others of their command. The troops all wore full field kits, their webbings hung with ammunition pouches, grenades, medical packs. The officers were similarly equipped, and as the troops reached their assigned places according to combat units, they were assembled for what immediately became clear to them would be detailed briefings. Unit leaders began to distribute small maps and prints of aerial photographs, showing lengths of a shoreline. The bright conversation and the grumblings about the remembered billetings at the training sites on the Isle of Wight lagged to an apprehensive silence. Several of the men remembered the clarity and windlessness of the afternoon sky they now could no longer see. The weather was ideal for a cross channel passage.

There was an abrupt moment of silence, too, a short time later in the wardroom of the destroyer Calpe, as vibrations surged through the ship, and the uniformed men heard other mechanical sounds and the muted calls of commands being issued from above deck. They became conscious of a slow stirring and knew the ship was moving away from her berth.

The sounds of voices, and some laughter, was taken up again in the wardroom, underscored now by the ship's engine vibrations. Stewards moved about clearing tables and refilling orders for drinks among the groups of men. Conversation was animated and cheerful, and there appeared an atmosphere almost of celebration now the ship was under way. The voices of the officers and men reflected a variety of dialects, British, Canadian, even American, and the conversations seemed pointedly concerned with anything except speculation about the hours just ahead. But beneath the spirited talk, the conversations of recent days and nights, of the almost holiday atmosphere of London during the weeks of that summer of 1942, the fears of a threatened German invasion now an almost forgotten thing, the increasing arrivals of American troops and Air Force units, beneath it all stirred a conscious awareness that a kind of waiting was finally coming to an end, had, in fact, ended with the Calpe moving out into the waters of Portsmouth harbor.

There had been earlier raids, of course. To Spitsbergen Island, to evacuate the Russian inhabitants to Archangel and then set afire the coal reserves before the Germans could make use of them; to the Lofotens, and the abortive raid on Hardelot, south of Boulogne, during which the recall rockets had been fired before the operation had actually been engaged, and Canadian troops involved in the raid had never even landed. There had been the Commando raid on the French port of St. Nazaire during the past spring. The drydock gates had been destroyed as planned, and the raid classified as successful despite the loss of so large a part of the raiding force. It had been the most ambitious operation mounted by Combined Operations Headquarters—until today.

Since the beginning of that year, the British had considered the possible alternatives in effecting diversionary operations along the coast of Western Europe designed to draw German forces away from the heavily engaged Russian front. The project had come under a code name, "Sledgehammer," and the Chiefs of Staff had directed the various internal commands, including Combined Operations, to implement projects that would make Germany maintain an active and continous major ground and air operational force in the West. In addition to air action, attacks by ground forces were considered, the possible establishment of a permanent bridgehead, or an enterprise of organized raids against the coasts. In April the British Chiefs of Staff issued a memorandum on "Operations on the Continent," which including the following directive on the subject of raids:

We have approved a policy of raids to be undertaken in the summer of 1942 on the largest scale that the available equipment will permit. These raids will be carried out on a front extending from the north of Norway to the Bay of Biscay and will be planned and launched by the Chief of Combined Operations in consultation with the Commander in Chief Home Forces.

It was an ambitious, and largely overextended view of the offensive capabilities of the forces then based in Great Britain. Combined Operations Headquarters had experience with small raids, employing limited strike forces and landing equipment that was at the time largely in developmental stages. They knew the operational potentials of the then-in-use infantry landing ships and assault and mechanized landing craft, but there were new types of craft, designed to deliver tanks and support artillery to beachheads, which had never been under fire. There was little more than theoretical appreciation of the handling of a force of numerous types of assault craft in conjunction with escort and support naval forces because, other than the unopposed landings in Madagascar in May, 1942, there had been no major assault landing attempted since the Gallipoli operation of World War I in 1915.

Numerous operations were discussed—a major raid on Alderney in the Channel Islands, an attack on the radar installation in the Cap de la Hague area near Cherbourg, even a bizarre plan of an armored raid on Paris, in which the raiding force would strike at one port and send an assault force against Paris to attack the German headquarters there. The raiders would then effect a retrograde along another route and withdraw from a different coastal point, with minor destructive attacks being accomplished at both ports of entry and exit. During that spring of planning, a succession of major operations were projected. Some even reached the stages of training and initial implementation. But only one major raid would actually be mounted...the Dieppe operation.

The target of Dieppe was chosen for numerous reasons: it would serve as a set piece for the primary objective then concerning planners of invasion operations, that being the assault and establishment of a beachhead on a major port. Dieppe, less than seventy miles across the Channel, was well within the effective range of fighter aircraft based at aerodromes in southeast England and could be afforded proper air cover and support. Intelligence reports had confirmed the existence of radar stations in the Dieppe area, and the frontage was considered to be not heavily defended. It was known also that forty landing barges were docked in the harbor of Dieppe. The German occupational division headquarters was located at Arques-la-Bataille, a short distance south of Dieppe, and could be effectively struck and plundered as part of the operation. And Dieppe, a resort town before the war, had a good open beachfront for assault approach. The adjacent coastline comprised largely unscalable cliffs, but there were gaps of beach at Pourville, two miles west of Dieppe, and at Puys, a mile to its east. The commanding headlands involved two major artillery batteries, at Berneval to the east, and Varengeville at the western extremity of the frontage of the planned assault. These batteries would have to be neutralized so that support naval craft could operate off the beaches.

A number of operational plans were produced, some of which included the use of parachute troops, gliders carrying airborne infantry to land and strike the nearby aerodrome installations at St. Aubin, and heavy preparatory aerial bombardment prior to the landing. Other contributing factors, such as the essential element of surprise, the importance of the port and harbor being taken undamaged, and the inability of air force planners to guarantee accuracy in preparatory bombardment of targets, all influenced the commanders to opt for a final operation plan that relied fundamentally on the factor of surprise. There was, as well, the factor of timing, the difficulties of organization and the feasibility of employing previously untried combat forces. Training could not begin before the final weeks of May, when the Headquarters 2nd Canadian Division arrived on the Isle of Wight as a vanguard for the troops that would take part in the raid, which was then scheduled to be mounted in the first week of July.

Now it was 19 August. The raid had been mounted and cancelled, then, for reasons that had tactical as well as political ramifications, mounted again. There was the need to mollify the enjoinders of the Russians who were increasingly calling for a second front in the West. The raid, originally planned to employ a largely Canadian force and then cancelled, threatened to undermine the morale of the Dominion troops who, but for minor participation in some of the earlier raids, had served in no combat capacity after close to three years on station in England. And there was, in the final planning stages, Operation "Torch," the Anglo-American invasion of French North Africa. There was the need to divert German attention from the continent of Africa. A ready-made plan with its force already trained provided the best possible operation for early deployment and likely success.

And there had, appropriately, been changes made in the plan. With the unpredictability of meteorological forecast, coupled to the requirement of ideal weather conditions, the use of parachute troops had been eliminated. In their place, Commando units would mount the strikes to destroy the flanking coastal batteries at either side of the Dieppe frontage. The command group had also met the need of change. Originally the responsible military authority had been the Commander in Chief of the Southeastern Command, Lieutenant General B. L. Montgomery, who in fact, had since been transferred to take command of the 8th Army in Egypt. Candian Major General H.D.G. Crerar was appointed in his place, with Air Vice Marshal Sir T. L. Leigh-Mallory and Vice Admiral Lord Louis Mountbatten of Combined Operations completing the supreme command group. Their representative field commanders were all on board the H.M.S. Calpe as she moved into the Portsmouth roadstead.

An array of communications equipment lined one wall of a large cabin on the Calpe's upper deck. A staff of operators was occupied with the instruments, and there were several senior officers also in the cabin, one wearing the uniform of a general officer of the Canadian army, another the deep blue of the Royal Air Force, and on whose sleeves were the chevrons of Air Commodore and the shoulder device identifying the officer as an Australian.

Major General J. H. Roberts spoke quietly with an aide, then returned his attention to a telephone receiver and a conversation with the naval force commander who was on the Calpe's bridge as she worked her way slowly into the roadstead in the deepening afternoon light. He nodded briefly and went to Air Commodore A.T. Cole, R.A.A.F., to whom he commented on affirmative signals that assigned minesweepers were already well into the Channel ahead of them. Both men then looked out across the waters, thinking of the hours ahead, and of the activities now going on among the vessels of this command. They knew that now the schedule was in movement, the ships were moving from their berths and briefings were being held in the wardrooms of the H.M.S. Queen Emma, the two other infantry landing ships here in Portsmouth, and among the support craft, the escort motor torpedo boats, assault ships, and the gunboat H.M.S. Locust. They watched the slow movements of the ships assuming positions, the sharp callings from the bridge penetrating their thoughts, the afternoon light fading rapidly now to early evening.

Air Commodore Cole thought deeply over the final decision to eliminate from the plan the heavy preparatory aerial bombardment of the assault beaches. It had been calculated that preservation of the harbor entrance and the roads at the edges of Dieppe was essential to the role the armor could play in supporting the assault force. The tanks could not deploy effectively through badly damaged roads or along deeply bombed beachfronts. So the Blenheims and the Hurricane bombers had been ordered to stand down, and the fighter cover would not begin until dawn. He then tried to count the ships forming up as parts of the force, but the light had grown too faint. He saw the flashing of an Aldis signal lamp from the bridge of a vessel alongside and realized that wireless communication had ceased. They would maintain radio silence now until the operation began. And this brought to mind his superior, Air Vice Marshal Leigh-Mallory, who, with General Crerar and Lord Louis Mountbatten, were waiting at their headquarters at Number 11 Fighter Group, R.A.F., at the fighter station at Uxbridge. He checked the time, it was 2120 hours, almost full darkness. If the schedule was maintained and timing held as planned, there would be no contact with Uxbridge now for just over seven hours. Considering the prospects of what lay ahead, he wondered whether, given the choice, he would prefer a posting at Uxbridge through this night, or be where he now was, in the operational headquarters ship. He knew, almost without thought, that he was exactly where he wanted to be. The waiting at least, would be easier. Once they were through the minefields, that is.

2

As final darkness fell over the waters before Portsmouth harbor, the fleet of ships assumed their dispersal points. Aldis lamps were flashing repeated signals, directing smaller craft to flotilla positions, their profiles barely recognizable now. The first of the ships cleared the defenses of the harbor at 2125 hours, precisely on schedule; it was the H.M.S. Queen Emma. She was followed by the other landing ships and the escort vessels, all now drawing into formation under command of the Calpe, on whose bridge now stood Captain John Hughes-Hallet, the naval force commander.

Captain Hughes-Hallet, Naval Adviser to Combined Operations Headquarters, had been part of the Dieppe planning group from its inception. He had objected to the planned frontal assault on the Dieppe beaches, regarding this phase of the plan as unduly hazardous, striking directly at beaches where the heaviest enemy defenses might be expected. It was decided ultimately that there were distinct advantages to the frontal assault. The Dieppe beach provided the best landing sites for the tanks, and would place them in immediate position to support the assaulting infantry. And by closely coordinating the timing of the flank attacks and the Commando strikes on the coastal batteries, the factor of advance warning to the main defenses within Dieppe would be minimized.

With the earlier cancellation of the operation, and its subsequent revival, there had been widely felt fears that the entire raid would be compromised by breaches in security. It was essential, therefore, to reactivate the operation with a sense of certainty that the Germans were not forewarned. It was known that the German air patrols had not been oblivious to the earlier massing of vessels. There had been the bombing raid during the July operation on the infantry landing ships in the Solent. Captain Hughes-Hallet had provided an acceptable solution. There was, he felt, no need to concentrate the entire force for embarkation. With the landing units trained as they were, they could be moved directly to embarkation points within hours of the actual departure. Some of the personnel landing craft, in fact, were of a size and seaworthiness to make the channel crossing safely, considering the weather forecasts. It was therefore decided that three of the main assault units would make the crossing in the vessels that would take them onto the beaches. This permitted further dispersal of the forces, who, it was decided, would embark from a number of different ports along the channel coast.

Including the units that sailed from Portsmouth, the force originated from five separate points. In addition to the Calpe, three infantry landing ships and numerous escort vessels sailed from Portsmouth. Others sailed from Gosport, and from the ports of Shoreham, Southampton and Newhaven. In addition to Calpe there were the "Hunt" Class destroyers Fernie, Brocklesby, Albrighton, Berkeley, Garth, and Bleadsdale. There was the Polish destroyer Slazak, the gunboat H.M.S. Locust, and the sloop Alresford. Six infantry landing ships sailed from Southampton, and two of the three personnel landing craft groups sailed from Newhaven, along with a contingent of tank landing craft. In all, the naval force was crossing the channel as thirteen individual groups, sailing at varying speeds, but all under the command of Captain Hughes-Hallet in the Calpe.

Hours earlier, sixteen craft of the Royal Navy's Ninth and Thirteenth Minesweeping Flotillas had moved out into the channel. It was toward the first marker light of the path they were clearing that the naval force now were making. Under a darkness in which the late rising moon had not yet appeared in the sky, the full force of 237 ships and landing craft set their carefully pre-determined courses out into the English Channel. Their destination was a stretch of water, ten miles off the French coast, fronting on the port of Dieppe.

The military force being carried by the flotilla totaled more than six thousand one hundred men. Most of them, nearly five thousand, were Canadians, more than one thousand were British commandos. There were some fifty Americans of the First U.S. Ranger Battalion, assigned through the various units as observers, and twenty men of the Number 10 (Inter-Allied) Commando. Most of these last were Frenchmen, and there were as well, several anti-Nazi enemy nationals who could expect to be executed if captured by the Germans.

The Canadians were represented by detachments of famous and romantically named regiments: the Royal Regiment of Canada, the Royal Hamilton Light Infantry, the Essex Scottish, and the Queen's Own Cameron Highlanders of Canada. There was the 14th Canadian Army Tank Regiment (the Calgary), the Toronto Scottish Machine Gun Regiment, Les Fusiliers Mont-Royal, who had been assigned the channel crossing in one of the landing craft groups, the Black Watch of Canada, the Calgary Highlanders, and the South Saskatchewan Regiment.

The British forces included the Royal Marine "A" Commando and the specialist force Commandos in two detachments, the Number 3, and the Number 4, commanded by the already famous Lieutenant Colonel Lord Lovat.

Now there were briefings being conducted among dozens of command groups dispersed through the naval force. Final signaling procedures were confirmed, and the identification from yesterday's Royal Air Force reconnaisance photographs were being carefully examined for the most recent identifiable German defense positions. The men were readying their weapons, Thompson .45 caliber submachine guns, Sten guns, Brens, PIATs. The weapons, all of which had been cleaned hours before, were cleaned and oiled again. Equipment checks were repeated, and once again, detailed re-briefings were given of the specific unit operations once the forces began the actual assaults on the beaches. The activities continued in a steady, animated atmosphere throughout the units into the night.

Some men among the troops quartered below-decks in the landing ships tried to read in what meager light there was. Others talked of London, of Canada, of two and a half years of Home Forces operations, of the mining of the beaches in Sussex and Kent, and of the stringing of the concertina wire and the other waterline defenses constructed against impending German invasion. They remembered the Engineer operations in Gibraltar, the massive anti-invasion training maneuvers of the Southeast Command in which the Canadians had taken part, and the famous exercise known as Exercise "Bumper," north and west of London, which had involved more than a quarter million troops, the largest military maneuver ever conducted in Great Britain.

The thirteen naval groups began to converge on an area in mid-channel, the lead position taken by Calpe and her force from Portsmouth. A wind had begun to blow lightly from the east, and a light mist carried swiftly on it into the bridges of the leading vessels. Men along the decks knew they were approaching the area of the German minefield and, throughout the ships, they began to don their life vests, the "Mae Wests" of R.A.F. fame. The yellow coloring of the vests made the men more visible to one another in the darkness, and added an almost inexplicable note of comfort among those lining the rails of Calpe's deck.

Finally, Calpe veered slightly in a small change of course, and word was passed quickly from the bridge. The watches had spotted the first of the minesweepers' vigil lights and they were beginning to pass through the minefield.

There was complete silence along the decks now as the men stared into the darkness, then, after a brief wait, saw the small deep green light. The speed with which Calpe sailed past startled some of the troops, and looking back they could not make out the shape of the ship directly following them, although they knew she was little more than one hundred yards astern. They returned their gazes to the darkened waters now, the quiet, misted night, and the suddenly ominous silence around them.

3

In the infantry landing ship Prince Albert, Lieutenant Colonel Lord Lovat and his Number 4 Commando were preparing for the assault on the most westerly target of the entire Dieppe Operation, the German coastal battery at Varengeville. The force included some two hundred and fifty men and a small detachment of the U.S. Ranger observers. The force was to be deployed in two landing parties and put ashore from assault craft. Their plan was to land on two beaches, "Orange I," and "Orange II." The first was a narrow beach at Vasterival, which was directly north of the German emplacement. It was to be approached and the battery engaged in direct exchange with mortars. Lord Lovat, commanding the larger landing force at "Orange II" Beach, would rush inland, make a detour and outflank the battery from the rear.

The attack was to jump off at 0450 hours, in direct conjunction with a parallel assault on the eastern coastal battery at Berneval. Number 3 British Commando would lead the attack at Beneval in a similarly designed assault at two points, "Yellow I" and "Yellow II."

The hour of the flank attacks, 0450, was calculated as the beginning of nautical twilight, and it allowed for the assault craft to touch down on the beach before true light.

Lord Lovat had participated in numerous small force raids prior to this. He had garnered an enviable reputation for not only his individual bravery, but for the fastidiousness of his operations and their remarkable success. The planning of the Commando operations had been the responsibility of their own unit commanders and they were entering the operation with due notation in the Order of Battle as "under command from Landing" only. The third Commando group, the Royal Marine "A" Commando, was posted as part of the floating reserve off the Dieppe beaches. Their operation was to enter Dieppe harbor after the seizure of the beachhead, remove as many of the German invasion barges as possible, then destroy the shipping remaining behind.

Including the two extreme flank assaults by Numbers 3 and 4 Commando, there were a total of five beach landings in the overall projected plan. On the inner flanks about the Dieppe beach, two attacks would secure the beaches at Pourville in the west, and Puys, east of Dieppe's harbor entrance. The Pourville landing, "Green" Beach, would be struck by a force of the South Saskatchewans commanded by Lieutenant Colonel C.C. I. Merritt. They would be followed thirty minutes later, when the beachhead was secured, by the Queen's Own Cameron Highlanders of Canada, commanded by Lieutenant Colonel A. C. Gostling, and would pass through the South Saskatchewans and link up with the main frontal attackers to strike through to the aerodrome at St. Aubin.

Simultaneous with the South Saskatchewan

landing at Pourville, the Royal Regiment of Canada would assault the beach at Puys, "Blue" Beach, under Lieutenant Colonel J. F. Durnford-Slater. Their specific orders, according to the Combined Plan stated: *The Royal Regiment of Canada at BLUE beach will secure the headland east of Dieppe (JUBILEE) and destroy local objectives consisting of machine gun posts, heavy and light flak installations and a four gun battery south and east of the town. The battalion will then come into reserve, and detach a company to protect an engineer demolition party operating in the gas works and power plant.*

The Royal Regiment had, in addition, three platoons of the Canadian Black Watch and detachments of the 3rd Light Anti-Aircraft Regiment and the 4th Field Regiment, which would capture and then man the enemy guns. This beach was of great importance in conjunction with the main attack on Dieppe. If this east headland was not completely neutralized, the weapons, in German hands, could have a clear field of fire on the main beaches of Dieppe.

At the same time as the Cameron Highlanders hit the Pourville beach in the second wave assault, the frontal assault was to be mounted, in two forces, on the beaches directly before Dieppe. The scheduled time was 0520 hours. On the right, the Royal Hamilton Light Infantry, under Lieutenant Colonel R. R. Labatt would assault "White" Beach, and on the left, "Red" Beach would be attacked by the Essex Scottish Regiment commanded by Lieutenant Colonel F. K. Jasperson. Simultaneous with the frontal assaults, nine tanks of the 14th Army Tank Regiment would be landed in the first wave.

In essence, the plan of operation was to effect the five landings successfully, take the port of Dieppe, and establish a defensive perimeter around the town while extensive demolitions were carried out. The Canadian engineer detachments were to "destroy the docks, swing bridges, harbor installations, rolling stock, power and gas works, and any other suitable objectives." The Royal Marine "A" Commando would then enter the harbor, man as many of the German invasion barges as possible, and bring them out for return to English ports. The remainder would be destroyed. The Queen's Own Cameron Highlanders would pass through the perimeter of Dieppe, join forces with the tank detachment and move inland to capture and destroy the aerodrome at St. Aubin. If the time schedule was maintained, the Highlanders were to then attack and capture the German divisional headquarters at Arques-la-Bataille. Finally, the floating reserve, Les Fusiliers Mont-Royal, would be put ashore as soon as the town was secure. They would occupy and maintain an inner perimeter and establish a rear guard action to cover the final withdrawal through Dieppe to the beaches.

The conditions governing the use of airborne troops or support forces in the form of parachute troops had been given considerable thought through the planning stages of the operation. The use of Numbers 3 and 4 Commando to assault the coastal batteries at Berneval and Varengeville was ultimately the decision taken in preference to airborne forces who, it was felt, could not be coordinated for properly timed landings in gliders because of the conditions of light that would prevail at the outset of the attack. The unpredictability of the weather, as stated earlier, dictated against the use of parachute troops. It was decided that it would be an entirely seaborne assault, with preparatory shoreline bombardment by the 4-inch guns of the destroyers to be timed in conjunction with the first flank assaults on the gun batteries. The coastline and beachfronts before Dieppe would come under the ten minute naval bombardment, to be lifted as the first wave moved into the beaches.

The coordination of the assaults and the central signals would be handled through the command vessel, the Calpe. A contigency headquarters was duplicated aboard the destroyer H.M.S. Fernie, its military commander being Brigadier C. C. Mann. Each headquarters ship also carried a Fighter Controller to direct the extensive air cover for the operation.

Aircraft from seventy four squadrons ultimately took part in the air support operations at Dieppe. There were forty eight fighter squadrons, of which five squadrons were in the air at any given time for general ground support and diversionary sweeps. Six squadrons of day bombers, Blenheims and Douglas A20 Bostons, two squadrons of Hurricane bombers, four additional squadrons for tactical reconnaisance, as well as intruder squadrons and three squadrons of smoke laying aircraft, all formed the air umbrella for the landing forces. The fighters were representative of most of the combat arms based on fighter stations in England at the time—the Royal Canadian Air Force, the Royal Air Force, the United States Army Air Force, and squadrons of the forces of New Zealand, Poland, Norway, Czechoslovakia, France, and Belgium.

Timed to coincide with the landings, four squadrons of U.S. Air Force B-17s, with an escort of 250 R.A.F. Spitfires, would attack the Luftwaffe fighter station on the aerodrome at Abbeville. This would disrupt enemy fighter operations in the area.

There were approximately 10,000 fighting men involved in the operations at Dieppe. Six thousand of these men were now finalizing their individual duties, steaming through the silent darkness of the Channel. The tensions roused in anticipation of the hours after dawn were raised to even greater levels because of the minefields through which the ships now threaded their way.

A small group of officers on the port deck of the Calpe spoke tightly to one another as the destroyer approached another of the minesweepers' vigil light buoys. The buoys had been dropped at half-mile intervals to mark the path swept through the minefield. For almost an hour now, the Calpe had been working her way on a course from one vigil light to the next. The ship's speed had relaxed somewhat through the minefield passage, and Calpe had executed numerous changes of course in the process. The minefield itself had been spotted by R.A.F. reconnaisance craft some days earlier, being set by German minelaying squadrons. A chance later reconnaisance had tracked a patrol of German E Boats working their way through the area, and on this observation, the minesweeping flotilla had steered the course to clear the path for the Calpe and the hundreds of ships in her wake.

Another of the vigil light buoys rushed past and, after several minutes, a signal chimed somewhere in the ship. A rush of voices rose in the darkness along the rails. The Calpe was through the minefield. The men heard the thin ringing of the engine telegraph from the bridge a short time after, the sound of the bow wave rose perceptibly as the destroyer raised her standard speed. The wind remained steady from the east, and a mist, or thin sea spray played about the deck.

And now they could see the moon, late risen and thin, through the covering haze. There were little more than fifty miles to sail before the force would disperse to the assault points, ten miles off the coast of the beaches surrounding Dieppe.

4

During the final hours before the attack was to be launched, the speed and positioning of the ships underwent considerable changes of course and organization. The infantry landing ships, which were the slowest of the craft in the flotilla, had to be in position off the coast within two hours of the attack time to disembark the assault landing craft. The smaller assault barges would be lowered ten miles off the French coast to avoid the possibility of radar detection by the German installation at Berneval. The assault craft would start toward the beaches immediately, two hours being allowed for the passage.

The large landing ships, with their naval escorts, moved into positions off the coast on schedule shortly before 0300 hours, and began lowering the landing craft with personnel aboard shortly afterward. The Prince Albert, off the coast at Varengeville, had carried Lord Lovat's Number 4 Commando. The Royals, farther east, were being disembarked from the Queen Emma and the Princess Astrid, while the ship Duke of Wellington carried the Black Watch detachment. All three hove-to off the coast at Puys and the assault groups were lowered to form up for the run in to the beaches. At Pourville, the landing ships Princess Beatrix and Invicta were deploying the South Saskatchewans, and off the beaches of Dieppe the Glengyle, Prince

Leopold, and Prince Charles effected the transfer of the Royal Hamilton Light Infantry and the Essex Scottish to the assault craft without incident.

The infantry landing ships then came about and began their return crossings to England.

Standing off the beaches at Dieppe, men aboard the Calpe could see the distant thin pulsing of the marker light in the lighthouse at the Dieppe harbor entrance. It was a sight that elicited a strange mixture of emotions—knowing the source of the light was an enemy position added to the tension, but at the same time, the rhythmic beacon being in operation was a certain and comforting sign that their presence was unsuspected. The assault craft hovered in groups, assuming formation under the smaller escort fighting craft that would accompany them on the run into the beaches.

The forces which had made the channel crossing in the large personnel landing craft, the Cameron Highlanders and Les Fusiliers Mont Royal, came up behind the main assault forces. Being floating reserves, or forces which were intended to land in a second wave on the Pourville beach, they would begin movement toward the beaches some time later. In the most easterly of the assault points, the force of Number 3 Commando, which had made the crossing from its embarkation point at Newhaven in 23 personnel landing craft, paused at the ten mile position to reorganize for the run in. They were escorted by a gunboat, an armed motor launch, and a landing craft armed as a flak ship. The eastern screening force of the destroyer Brocklesby and the Polish fighting ship Slazak stood off the coast in position as Number 3 Commando began to move toward the beaches at 0300 hours.

Ranged out to the west and east of H.M.S. Calpe at that critical hour of 0300, over a ten mile frontage facing the coast, the hundreds of ships and landing craft had formed their final assault positions. The wind had died as the force had approached the coast and sitting now across the calm, misted waters, the officers and men of the landing forces strained to see through the darkness their first sign of the beaches they would strike with the coming dawn. Off Dieppe the men could, of course, see the dim signal beacon of the harbor lighthouse. The sounds of equipment and ship movements during the lowering operations had appeared deafening in the dark and it seemed incredible that the sounds had not carried across to warn the shore forces. But after the long minutes of the transfers and the moving away of the infantry landing ships, the surface of the channel had returned to silence.

And into the silence the first assault craft began their runs, the men readying their weapons, camouflaging their faces and arms with blacking, steadying their tensions with self repetition of orders and instructions—the color codes of beaches, objectives, time schedules, signal codes, the names and time sequences of the coastal points they could not yet see in the darkness—the prospects of whether they would survive the following hours after dawn.

The crossing and the initial dispersals had gone off perfectly. The good fortune and detailed planning that had brought the force across the channel need only continue now for a few more hours. It was clear that the Germans had not been expecting the raid. The closer the time drew to the moment of touchdown, the more confident the landing forces grew that this massive assault, the first contact with the enemy on Continental soil by Canadians and United States forces, however few, would be a staggering blow to the Germans' supposedly impregnable coastal defense system. The first aggressive military operation of major size by forces in the West, it would give a needed boost to the morale of the Allies, in England and across the Atlantic in America and Canada, who had been waiting long now for signs of a turning point in the war.

The longer the silence, the greater the optimism grew through the command group. Soon the sense of isolation among the forces out here off the coast of France would be broken by the arrival of the first of the air force cover operations. At 0515 hours, just after the initial flank assaults would begin, five squadrons of Hurricanes were to make a cannon attack on the beach defenses at Dieppe, and shortly afterward the sky would be covered by the umbrella of fighters that would protect landing parties and naval support groups from air attack. Wireless contact with the overall command at Uxbridge could be commenced at dawn and the full effectiveness of Combined Operations would come powerfully into play in support of the landing strike forces.

Off the points of the five landing sites, the assault craft moved closer to shore. Almost half of the two hour run-in had passed and everything continued on split-second schedule. The two waves of Lord Lovat's Number 4 Commando were moving toward "Orange I" and "Orange II" Beaches. Major D. Mills-Roberts, leading the frontal assault group into the beach at Vasterival, stared into the darkness, hoping that the naval officer who commanded his group of landing craft was on target. The beach at Vasterival was very narrow, under commanding cliffs directly north of the coastal battery. His 88 man force were to scale the cliff, advance toward the battery, and open diversionary fire with small arms and a 2-inch mortar. The point of touchdown was of critical importance. There had to be time for the force to get to the cliff crest and begin the diversion before Lord Lovat's main force began their assault from the flank landing at "Orange II." The darkness still shrouded the beaches ahead and the force moved closer to shore.

At the eastern extreme of the operation, Lieutenant Colonel Durnford-Slater's Number 3 Commando also moved toward the beaches in total silence. It was now 0340 hours. Lieutenant Colonel Durnford-Slater kept close control of the time and knew he would soon order the craft to divide into the two attack groups for landing at the two indicated beaches, "Yellow I" and "Yellow II." At 0345 he was preparing to order the division of the landing craft force when he was suddenly alerted by the naval officer commanding his craft of a movement across the water by a craft that could not be identified.

Number 3 Commando had run into an encounter that had had its origins at the port of Boulogne long hours before. The beginning of the battle at Dieppe, which had been unplanned and which would have significant consequences for the entire operation, was only minutes away. A silent and frustrating drama, that had been played in the communications rooms of the Naval Station at Portsmouth for some hours now, was about to culminate here on the waters off the coast of Berneval.

Lieutenant Colonel Durnford-Slater rose to the small bridge of the landing craft and joined the naval officer in command. Together the men glassed the area east and north of the assault craft flotilla. It was silent and dark once again, nothing showing across the waters. The wash of the waters beneath the landing craft's bow overrode any sound, but through the darkness, the shape of another L.C.P. showed close by. The Colonel knew the escort gunboat was stationed off the port side of his craft. He was certain the naval lieutenant had mistaken the gunboat for the "unidentifiable" craft he had reported moments before. He continued to watch the darkness over the north side of his flotilla. Half a minute passed, and he checked the time again. It was coming up on the moment to order the division of the force for the final run. He looked up again just as the first explosion of gunfire hammered into the darkness. In the yellow flash and the red tracers that arched across the blackness, he saw one of the personnel landing craft erupt in flames. In the spill of the sudden light, he made out the shape of a German E Boat moving toward his group of landing craft.

5

A small German coastal convoy had sailed south from Boulogne at 2000 hours the night before, 18 August, close to the time the flotilla under Calpe's command was forming up for the channel crossing from the English ports.

Moving slowly through the calm waters, the five German motor sailing vessels were under escort by a minesweeper and two fast motor chase vessels, the 120 foot long E Boats, carrying their normal armament in addition to torpedoes, 50-caliber machine guns, and anti-aircraft weapons. The motor sailing vessels were carrying the cargo of a routine garrison supply convoy and they hugged the coast in the darkness, slowly passing the scheduled coastal points, Le Touquet, Berck-Plage, and the broad estuary of the Somme with its coastal towns of Le Crotay and Gayeux-sur-Mer. Somewhere off the coast near Le Treport, the convoy changed its heading, still following the coast, to west-southwest. It was after midnight, and they were moving into their final run along the coast to their port of destination, the Gare Maritime at Dieppe.

The change of course took them some distance farther from the coast. At a point almost eight miles out, the watches began glassing the horizon for the first signs of the expected coastal markers at Criel-Plage and Biville. This would bring them along the coast to within sighting of the marker beacon of the Dieppe lighthouse, some three hours sailing distance. Dimmed because of the security conditions in effect along the Channel, the Dieppe marker light was still operating for use by coastal vessels. It was felt that existing security systems and the distance across the Channel from the English coast provided sufficient marginal safety to allow retention of so important a navigational aid for maritime traffic under German command.

With the minesweeper setting the course, the five small cargo ships maintained a close line-astern formation. The E boats moved along the flanks of the convoy, their low-throttled engines rumbling deeply. The watches relaxed as fix points were made on Criel-Plage. They were on schedule, they knew now, and they were sailing through a quiet length of coast. There had been few convoy attacks along this length of coast through the past year. The outer minefields had kept the Royal Navy patrols beyond the coastal shipping lanes and the British night fighters were not known to operate against Channel shipping. The British were also known to have not committed a capital ship to duty in the Channel. So there was little or no fear of coming under long range gunfire.

The German minesweeper helmsman checked his course in relation to the Criel-Plage fix, and the ship's commander cleared with the watches that the convoy vessels were maintaining their positions. The thin moon allowed for a limited visiblity as the craft continued to follow the coast.

At about the time the German convoy had

changed course, the Commander-in-Chief at Portsmouth, some eighty miles across the Channel, was advised that movements by eight unidentified vessels were being traced on a heading of west-southwest along the French coast, closing on the waters around Dieppe. The movements reflected on the radar screen were followed for a short tense time, the operators checking and rechecking their instruments and readings. Finally, on advisement by the Commander, warning signals were issued, breaching radio silence, to the force commander on board Calpe, at 0127 hours, reporting the presence of small craft.

There was no acknowledgement of the warning call.

Portsmouth could not know if the signals had been received, and the Calpe, not wishing to compromise radio silence, merely decided not to acknowledge the warning. The Calpe, in fact, had not received the warning call.

Portsmouth repeated the warning signal at 0244 hours. The unidentified craft were maintaining their heading and were approaching the waters where it was known the raiding craft were now beginning to assemble in preparation for the assault. Again the response from the darkened waters of the Channel was silence.

There was silence, too, at Headquarters, Number 11 Fighter Group, R. A. F., at the station at Uxbridge. Portsmouth had advised Combined Operations Headquarters at its command field unit of the observation of unidentified craft, and of the warning signals that had been transmitted. 0300 hours had come and passed now, and those familiar with the specifics of the operational order knew that nothing but waiting could be done now. Within the operational order, one critical comment stated: "If the operation has to be cancelled after the force has sailed, the decision must be made before 0300 hours." It was impossible to call off the operation once the landing craft were in the water. Breaching radio silence after the 0300 time would totally compromise the operation at its most vulnerable stage, since the landing ships were already on their return passage to England.

There was the chance, of course, that the unidentified craft, while operating within the vicinity of the raiding force, would miss any contact. The command group at Uxbridge waited in tense silence as the time approached for the scheduled touch downs on the beaches and the reestablishment of radio contact with the operational command on board Calpe. The coordinating controller advised that the Hurricane fighters scheduled to attack the beaches at Dieppe had completed briefings and were awaiting final clearance for departure from their stations.

Commander D.B. Wyburd, the Group Commander of the naval escort force accompanying Lieutenant Colonel Durnford-Slater's Number 3 Commando, was aware, within minutes of the confrontation with the German convoy, of the naval order within his specific commands. It directed that radio silence might be broken "By Senior Officer of Group 5 (Commander Wyburd) if by delays or casualties it is the opinion of the senior military officer that the success of the landing at 'Yellow' Beach is seriously jeopardized."

By the time he had reached his decision, only moments after the beginnings of the gunfire, the communications equipment on his gunboat had been destroyed by a direct hit from one of the E boats. The sky was alight across the entire group of assault craft within moments, and the ending minutes of the night had suddenly, and disastrously, come apart.

6

Number 3 Commando, in the 23 personnel landing craft, were still one hour away from touchdown when the E boat struck. The initial gunfire targeted the E boat and the British gunboat began to return fire even as the E boat moved rapidly toward direct contact with the landing craft group. Small arms from all the landing craft began to fire and in the flashes, the Commandos could see, across the water, the concentration of the German convoy. Tracers began to fly at them from farther back. Racing across the convoy group toward them, a second German vessel opened up its bow guns.

The wireless station along the bridge of Commander Wyburd's gunboat took a direct hit, and control of the craft was lost for a brief moment. Fires had erupted along the small fighting boat's forward deck and in its light, the commander saw his forward gun crew firing steadily at the oncoming E boat. He watched for the register of shells, the tracers of the E boat's machine guns passing over in red and green flashes. An orange flash was followed by a sudden eruption that seemed to cause the gunboat to lose steerageway. The whole ship bucked and the fires along the forward deck suddenly died to a dark smouldering glow. But the forward gunners were still firing at the oncoming motor torpedo boat. A new brightness suddenly lit the night to starboard and looking there, the commander saw one of the Commando assault craft rise slightly from the surface of the water, then settle and begin to burn furiously.

The formation of assault craft had broken and there were small ships in all directions now, with traces of gunfire playing from all of them.

The commander knew the sounds and flashes of the gunfire had carried across to where H.M.S. Calpe stood hove-to, and his immediate action was to attempt to signal for cover fire from the nearest destroyer screening force, the Brocklesby and the Slazak.

On deck he ordered a signalman to flash to the motor launch that the wireless was inoperable and that word be transmitted of the contact with the enemy. The launch had maneuvered close alongside to form a screening force to protect the landing craft. The oncoming E boat had executed a turn to starboard and was bringing its full broadside gunnery into action against them. The gunboat's forward gunners found their target in that moment, and the E boat's forward movement died. The German boat was stilled and suddenly rocked by repeated explosions and white flashes. The air began to be clouded with smoke and the acrid smells of gunfire. There were fires burning across the water now in numerous places.

Lieutenant Colonel Durnford-Slater watched from his post on the small bridge of his landing craft, able to see the light of fires between the shapes of the screening naval boats. From either side he heard gunfire from the men in the landing craft, but the sounds now were growing more distant. The sudden sea fight was spreading widely across the water, the light flashes of the gunfire being reduced to ever widening points. He looked around, trying to locate the craft carrying his forces, but was able to locate only one, the craft that had taken the first hits and which was now afire and grimly silent.

On board the motor launch, the signal to establish radio contact with the force commander had been seen. The wireless silence now broken across the sea frontage by the sound and sight of this first encounter, the sudden rush of radio traffic prevented the launch's operator from establishing audible contact with Calpe, or, for that matter, any other of the screening vessels. The escort ships of Group 5, without additional support available, continued the exchanges of gunfire with the remaining E boat and the minesweeper, whose guns had by now come into action.

Brocklesby and Slazak, laying off the coast farther to the west, had observed signs of the action in the distance, the senior commander of the screening force deciding that the gunfire had come from installations on shore. Communication efforts with the escort of Number 3 Commando failing, a report of observed action was made to the headquarters ship, with orders received to steam toward the source of observed gunfire and investigate. But the easterly screening destroyers were too late. The assault craft of Number 3 Commando had become completely scattered.

Several of the craft had been severely damaged during the opening minutes of the fight. A fire still burned on board one of the small landing craft. And the force commander within his own craft could not know the condition of the assault force, or, indeed, how much of it remained afloat. The cargo vessels of the German convoy had retired directly from the scene of the battle and, beyond the damaged escort craft nearby, none of the enemy could now be seen, save for the burning E boat that had settled visibly deeper into the water.

The sky was beginning to show the first signs of morning light now, and Commander Durnford-Slater, aware that his assault group had been completely disrupted and the enemy on shore quite obviously forewarned, fought with the decision he knew he would have to make—the issue of orders, by whatever means possible, that the assault by Number 3 Commando be stood down. He stood on the bridge of his damaged assault craft and looked across the waters, weighing heavily the alternatives available to him, and, more largely, the effect this would have on the entire operation.

The sea fight had ended as abruptly as it had begun, but its aftermath was a scene of wide-ranging disorder. Instead of a tightly controlled flotilla of twenty three personnel landing craft with escort, only the flak craft and the gunboat were visible. Smoke trailed across the water from the burning gunboat, and from the fires on the smaller craft. The few assault craft within his range of sight had obviously been seriously damaged.

As the sky lightened, the force slowly effected a reorganization. They could hear, in the distance to the west, the gunfire of the other attacks beginning. The sky above them suddenly showed the shadows of aircraft, the droning sounds rising at speeds these men, who had been hours in slow moving craft on the waters, could not at once reconcile. The first fear of enemy air attack vanished quickly as the recognizable silhouette of a Spitfire came in low, roared over them, then banked and turned toward the beaches. Other fighters began to circle the broken group, and from the slowly collecting remnant of the group of assault craft, shouts of greeting were called across the water.

Aside from Lieutenant Colonel Durnford Slater's craft, fifteen of the L.C.P.s remained, and most of these were damaged. There were numerous wounded on board, and several of the craft were barely seaworthy. The commander of the gunboat located the group commander and the wounded were taken off the smaller craft. Lieutenant Colonel Durnford Slater had made his decision. The assault on "Yellow I" and "Yellow II" Beaches was cancelled, and the following hour was spent organizing the flotilla for a return crossing to England.

The Commando force leader would report to General Roberts on the headquarters ship before long and would return to England without knowing that any of the men of Number 3 Commando had, in fact, landed at the Berneval beaches. The seven unaccounted for assault craft would, indeed, land their troops along the "Yellow" beaches, and would engage a battle that was ultimately described in the report of Captain Hughes-Hallet as: "in my judgment...perhaps the most outstanding incident of the operation."

7

The force commanders on board the Calpe had seen and heard the signs of contact with the Germans to the east, but all efforts to establish communication with the Number 3 Commando had failed. Before the flashes of gunfire had finally stopped, Calpe moved in closer to shore. Signals to the Brocklesby and Slazak by Aldis lamp had sent the eastern screening escort ships to investigate the source of the firing.

The men had seen what appeared to be anti-aircraft tracers rising above the distant scene of fighting, and speculation rose that the Germans' radio sounding devices had confused the engine sounds of the motor torpedo boats with aircraft. But, now that dawn was coming and light streaked the eastern sky, it became clear that the fighting, whatever its source, had had a slowing effect on the approach of the Royal Regiment of Canada toward the beaches at Puys. If they did not land shortly, they would touch down in full daylight. The Royals were the units closest to the fighting that had taken place between the German convoy and Number 3 Commando, and with no report of touchdown at 0450, it was assumed the earlier encounter had been the cause. This gave further cause to the belief that what had been witnessed was anti-aircraft fire, directed mistakenly at the incoming assault craft.

Actually, the delay caused in the landings at Puys derived from difficulties during the transfer of troops to the assault craft, and not because of the sea fight to the east. It ultimately caused the Royals to reach the beach after light, with tragic consequences.

The landings at "Green" Beach, near Pourville, came off with almost split second accuracy, the units of the South Saskatchewans reaching the beaches unobserved. But they had been landed in the wrong place. The beach at Pourville is bisected by the mouth of the River Scie, which empties into the Channel there. It was planned for the Saskatchewans to be landed east of the beach, so their assault could flow into a direct flanking support of the thrust against the main beaches of Dieppe. Landing as they did, west of the river, added the difficulty of occupying the high ground and passing through the village of Pourville, then crossing a bridge which carried the road east to Dieppe. The delays ultimately made the successful and unobserved landing have little meaning in terms of tactical contribution to the overall objectives of the raid.

At the extreme western flank of the operation, Number 4 Commando moved in toward the beaches designated "Orange I" and "Orange II" precisely on schedule. Lord Lovat's force of 250 British Commandos and the U.S. Rangers was put ashore completely unobserved and still under the cover of the near-dawn darkness.

At "Orange I" Beach, Major D. Mills-Roberts led the smaller eighty-eight man force away from the assault craft and quickly across the narrow beach. Overhead, the cliffs at the head of the beach rose steeply, and against the lightening sky the men could see the broken lace pattern of barbed wire. The men began the long tortuous climb along the steep faces of the cliff. From the east they then heard the distant sounds of gunfire. The Saskatchewans at Pourville had run into German gunners. To the Commandos this meant the Germans manning the batteries above them had by now been alerted. The scaling operations were hurried, men using special equipment working their way higher along the cliff face, preparing paths by which the others could follow quickly. Finally, grappling hooks were thrown and secured on points just below the barbed wire emplacements and the first troops of Major Mills-Roberts' force raised themselves carefully over the crest of the cliff.

Once at the crest, the commandos saw that the wire obstacles were more extensive than they had appeared from below. Men with cutters went to work silently. The remainder of the force completed the climb, armourers carrying with them the elements of the 2-inch mortar. The men massed at the crest of the cliff, but officers ordered the troops to fan out. Men with cutters began working at the densely constructed wire obstacles at several points farther out, and the rest of the force moved quietly to places of cover now that the light was coming.

Major Mills-Roberts scanned the beaches to the west, looking for signs of Lord Lovat's landing force. The shape and configuration of the cliffs obscured the view to the western portions of the beach. "Orange II" was beyond a point and a little more than a mile southwest along the coast. He was unable to see the point, but did notice no sign of craft on the water. To him it meant the force had landed with the same precision as had his own. There was also no sign or sound of any fighting from the westerly direction.

In the east, from the area of Pourville, there was continued firing. Too much firing. Looking briefly out over the water in the direction of the main force, Mills-Roberts could now see groupings of ships and landing craft. He saw the craft carrying the second wave that was scheduled to land at Pourville, the Cameron Highlanders. They were some distance out from the beach, perhaps three miles. He knew now there was little time to lose in engaging the battery of 6-inch guns just south of his position. The batteries, if brought to bear within the next few minutes, could blow the entire force of Camerons out of the water. The escort ships would have little chance, as well, under the 6-inch guns.

The men were through the wire and still unobserved. Now the command group of Number 4 Commando moved north away from the crest of the cliff, the men of the force spreading out once through the wire and deploying as assault teams for the move on the battery. Stopping briefly as the light rose to a sudden morning brightness, one officer raised his glasses to scan the high headland. As he screwed the eyepieces into focus, the lenses brought the distant details into sharp clear focus—he was looking at the concrete platforms on which were mounted the massive 6-inch coastal artillery pieces. While he studied the guns, he heard the first of the gunfire of the Commando small arms and the sudden tearing sound of a German machine gun.

The men dropped to crouched positions as they moved forward, stopping to fire, moving and then firing again, the force spreading wide to draw fire to all sides while the mortar crew set up the base plate and guide tube and prepared the weapon for firing. Ammunition was carried up to the mortar position as the gunner completed preparations, laying for elevation and cross leveling. The interlace of the German machine gunners increased as the light brightened to full daylight.

It had taken the force just over an hour since touch-down to scale the cliff and cut through the wire obstacles. It was almost 0600 hours now. In twenty minutes an attack was scheduled by cannon firing fighters. The force had to prevent the batteries from commencing fire until at least then.

Finally, the mortar fired its first round. It landed far short and the gunner had to change the elevation. The breeches of the 6-inch guns were moving now, and the support infantrymen of the Commandos moved closer under the machine gun fire, closing the range so they could lay down a more accurate fire pattern into the gun positions. A pall of smoke hung low over the fighting now, obscuring the targets. But the men were able to see there was no movement from the German gun positions. They shifted squads from low cover to a series of outcrops higher along the rise toward the batteries. The Germans had obviously not anticipated the likelihood of an assault from beneath the cliff, and, beyond the construction of the elaborate barbed wire fortification, had not cleared the elevation leading to the battery frontage. The cover available was low, but relatively adequate, until within fifty or sixty yards from the foot of the actual battery structure.

A curious light played over the battery, a mixture of the smoke of gunfire and the rapidly changing shades of the first minutes of the new morning. Looking back and out to sea, several of the men saw a high flight of aircraft. They began to call out, thinking it to be the expected fighter sortie, as the mortar began firing again. The 2-inch weapon lay down a pattern of three rounds, straddling the concrete fortification behind which the German gun crews had taken cover. The return fire intensified and several of the troops, having moved closer under the battery positions, began throwing grenades, most of which landed short of the battery.

Two platoons had moved up along the flank using carefully positioned Bren gunners to lay down cover fire and draw attention from the machine gunners, who had by now begun to inflict casualties among the Commando troops and kept them pinned to their positions of cover. It came to one lieutenant in those minutes, that this force had attacked the battery from the least defended flank. He knew there must be extensive gun emplacements along the western side of the headland, the rise along which Lord Lovat was to lead the main force. As he led his platoon from one place of cover to the next, the light changing constantly in the haze of smoke that hung in the windless air, the first gun of the German battery fired a salvo. The blast was deafening and the shock wave of the shell passing overhead could be felt all across the northern headland. The report of the salvo was underscored by a mortar round, then a second. Through this, the west flank platoon made its rush toward a German machine gun emplacement.

The lieutenant turned to a man moving beside him and made to signal a change in direction. The man was thrown backward as he raised an arm, and the lieutenant saw the detention handle of the grenade fly out as the armed grenade fell from the dead trooper's hand. He threw himself to the ground just an instant before the detonation. He was sure, at that instant, that he had heard the roar of an aircraft engine pass overhead, but he did not look up. Another grenade exploded close by, followed by heavy gunfire. The lieutenant moved then, rising to his knees and bringing his Sten gun to his waist as he began running, firing as he raced forward, the sights before his eyes moving swiftly and joltingly as a result of his movements. There was a trace of flame from the direction of the machine gun emplacement. He realized then that the German position was not firing. He rushed up to the emplacement, reaching it just as two other troops did. The three men jumped to cover in what remained of the protective cover of the German position. Along the headland, the firing continued steadily and the mortar continued to drop rounds onto the position of the 6-inch guns. None of the guns had fired after the first salvo.

The dead Germans in the machine gun emplacement were still bleeding, and the lieutenant, thinking one of them to be still alive, fired his Sten gun at point blank range at the German's chest. His vision was blurred in that instant, and again he could hear the sound of aircraft overhead. The men looked up, and over the sound of the still firing mortar they heard the repeated roars of aircraft engines.

The sounds of the small arms, the aircraft, even the rhythmic explosion of the mortar rounds was suddenly drowned by a huge detonation. They were certain at the moment that the 6-inch gun had fired another salvo. But looking up they saw a series of flames tear out from the position of the German gun battery. Smoke thickened heavily. There was a noticeable decrease in the sound of the small arms firing immediately after, and troops of the Commando unit began to leave their cover and move forward, closer to the battery emplacement.

High overhead, covering fighter aircraft began to circle. The air cover had flown in across the channel. The lieutenant, lying in the cover of the destroyed German emplacement, looked across the open headland and saw others of the force stop firing briefly to look up at the circling fighters. He glanced toward the now silent battery, and in the instant saw the movement toward his left—a short chopping movement as if something was being raised and lowered repeatedly.

They are going to come out at us, he thought suddenly, hardly knowing why the idea of a counterattack had come to him in that moment.

What he had seen and only understood on the instinct of his combat experience, was the movement of uniformed figures in close file, jumping from a high place of concealment to a lower point. He signaled the men of his platoon and moved out and back in the direction of the barbed wire.

The batteries had been immobilized by the explosion they had just seen, and looking back, the lieutenant realized the covering force of the battery was moving out to try flanking the attacking force and strike the mortar position from the rear. It did not matter, he realized suddenly. Whatever had happened, the guns of the battery were not firing. Now was the time to move. He spoke quickly with a squad leader, then moved out toward the unit command post.

The firing began just back of them as the Commandos moved up and began the final rush toward the side openings of the gun battery. The area was still dense with smoke. The troops fell to new cover within short range of the emplacement, then began concentrating their fire to draw full attention away from the far quarter. It was just moments short of the time scheduled for the cannon fighters to come in. The command post had been moved up with the unit rush and a rear guard of Bren gunners and other troops lay back of the old position, waiting for the movement of the flanking German units.

Before the fighters arrived, the men of Colonel Mills-Roberts' force heard the distant beginning of the battle as Lord Lovat and the main force began the assault from the west.

Then the fighters struck. The men took cover as the low-level attack began. They were Hurricanes and they came in straight from over the water, using the smoke of the earlier explosion as a target marker. A string of explosions laced over the battery emplacement as the 20-millimeter cannon fire of the first craft struck. It followed in a pattern after that, a brief pause as one aircraft passed and the next made its run, the mound of smoke about the battery position widening and rising. Beneath the sound of the cannon and the hammering of the aircraft overhead, the sound of Bren gunners came from back of the Commando positions. The troops were all firing now, and few could find clearance to look back. The low hanging smoke was so dense now that visibility had come down to little more than ten yards, except for directly overhead. The Hurricanes kept coming in, the cannon fire spreading wider now, enfilading the entire southern section of the headland. Then, as suddenly as it had begun, the sound of the aircraft stopped.

Moving up from southwest of the headland, the men of Lord Lovat's force watched the air attack from positions where they had been pinned down by accurate German machine gun crossfire. The casualties had begun to mount now that the men were moving in full morning light. The strike by the Hurricanes seemed to divert the German gunners and the men moved up again in small units, maintaining the tempo of movement, refusing to be stopped as they approached the long headland. They had crossed a coastal road after coming off the beach in the dark. They could see a more easterly section of the road now, which passed just beneath the position of high ground that was now being pounded by the Hurricanes. Below and closer to their lines of movement, there were fieldwork obstructions and the incessant sounds of machine guns.

The air attack ranged off and this served as a signal for a massive rush forward by the major assault force of Number 4 Commando. Two companies mounted the ridges that paralleled the road, and other units moved up directly under the fieldworks. The men began to fall, some hit as they placed charges to destroy the obstacles, others while moving toward the final space of open ground that surrounded the battery. But the momentum of the moving assault forces continued.

As the first troops approached the open ground, four men were struck and fell almost simultaneously. Two of them were the unit's officers. Another officer, Captain P.A. Porteous, already wounded but still moving forward, struggled to the position of the fallen men. He urged the remaining men forward, and taking the lead, rushed out across the open ground. He was seen to stop briefly, stagger, then rouse himself and continue forward, holding the point position of his force as they stormed across the last of the open ground, dashed across the road, and plunged into the perimeter defenses of the battery, his Sten gun firing.

After the cannon Hurricane attack, it seemed incredible that Germans were still alive and fighting, but this was very much the case. Captain Porteous and his lead troop, joined by the rest of Lord Lovat's point force, now stormed the close-in positions and brought their full gunfire to bear on the troops within the battery complex. Back of them, machine gun fire could still be heard out along the slope. They had stormed the outer perimeter defenses, bypassed machine gun emplacements, and were fighting now at the central point of the battle.

The familiar sound of Sten guns was heard beyond the area of battle and they knew the men of Lieutenant Colonel Mills-Roberts force were moving up from the rear. The order was given to fix bayonets. Germans were moving to defilade positions, and gunfire was coming into the area from outer perimeter points. An order rang out and the men moved forward in a final rush, dashing into the blinding smoke that filled the battery area, thrusting their weapons, firing, moving, always moving.

Suddenly the area fell to silence. Captain Porteous looked around him, surprised that he was still standing. He had been wounded again after the final rush, but was not yet aware of any pain.

He was afterward awarded the Victoria Cross.

Beneath the sounds of scattered gunfire back along the ridges, the engineers moved through the battery and planted charges. The force moved out, back along the ridge toward "Orange II" Beach, paused while the charges were detonated, and saw the entire battery disappear beneath a cloud of black smoke and orange streaks of flame. Debris from the explosion fell as far back as some of the troops were who had escorted the engineers out from the position. Below them there were still the sounds of machine guns firing. They knew they would have to fight their way back to the beach.

Reinforcements had been brought up along the road from the coastal village of Quiberville. The Germans had established mortar positions over "Orange II" Beach, and in the running fight that the retrograde action became, several more casualties were suffered by the Commando force.

As the men dashed across the beach to the waiting assault craft, they ducked under the covering fire coming from the gunners in the craft. Then a lone German fighter, which had broken through the upper air cover, made a low sweeping, strafing attack across the beach.

To keep from grounding, the assault craft had stood off about ten yards from shore. The Commandos waded out carrying their wounded, mounted the craft, their faces gray, their eyes lifeless. The Focke-Wulf made several more passes across the craft as they retreated from the shoreline, and mortar rounds were still dropping along the beach they had just crossed. Moving out, several of the men looked back. They could see the figures of fallen troops lining the beach. The men in the craft were still firing back at the shore, but the German fighter had vanished. It was 0730 hours. Four German prisoners huddled low against the bulwarks in one of the assault craft. The units moved out from the smoke filled shoreline, now out of range of the German guns. They were picked up by various escort craft, and one of the assault craft somehow even found its way to the side of H.M.S. Calpe. They had lost contact with their force and blundered across the channel frontage into the flotilla supporting the main thrust at Dieppe.

At 0850 hours, Lord Lovat reported to the headquarters ship and sent an unorthodox report to the Chief of Combined Operations, "Every one of gun crews finished with bayonet. OK by you?"

Number 4 Commando had suffered more than forty five casualties, including twelve men killed. The action, however, had been completely successful and had achieved its full objectives, the taking of the Varengeville battery, the destruction of the 6-inch gun emplacements, and the bringing off of prisoners.

It was the only successful action of the entire Dieppe operation.

8

As the sea fight which had engulfed Lieutenant Colonel Durnford-Slater's Number 3 Commando raged over the spreading area of water, the gunfire and the tracer patterns rising lazily in the pre-dawn sky off the eastern beaches of Berneval served as concealment for a small part of the force. Seven of the Commando's landing craft had avoided the battle and continued moving south over the water toward their points of touch-down along the "Yellow" Beaches.

Five of the craft, whose target beach was "Yellow I," maintained contact through the final run. They were overtaken by the damaged motor launch, which had lost contact in the final moments of the action with the E boats. With the launch (ML 346) as escort, the force approached the beach off Petit Berneval, northeast of the coastal battery on the heights above.

The light of the dawn spread across the beaches while the craft were still well offshore, and as the headland came into clear silhouette beneath the early sky, tracers of gunfire arced out over the water toward the landing craft. The armed launch moved ahead, its machine gunners opening a return fire toward the beach.

Looking back briefly, the launch's commander saw a sixth landing craft moving up in the wake of the group of five he was escorting. The five L.C.P.s were moving out into a formation abreast now, approaching the beach. There was a low curl of surf into which the first of the craft moved, its broad flat shape rising at the bow, then dropping steeply. The launch moved ahead, coming broadside to the beach. Racing west in a covering maneuver just back of the beaching craft, the launch brought its port machine guns into firing position on the lower points of enemy gunfire from the beach. The men in the bow of the landing craft were firing small arms now, and as the first craft beached, the launch slowed and its gunners concentrated their fire directly over the section of beach where the craft had touched down.

"Yellow I" Beach traced along a broad slope to its high water mark, then rose steeply to the first of several terrace-like dunes. The front ramp of the landing craft came down and the first of the troops jumped onto the beach. They were moving from the instant they hit the beach, the concentration of German machine gun fire directed now at the open bow of the craft. One troop leader had touched another man's shoulder encouragingly as they moved forward to disembark and felt the man go limp before he had released his grip. He looked down and made to go to the man's aid, but he was forced forward by the surge of others coming from behind. He lost his footing as he dropped from the edge of the ramp. He was up and running at once, tracing a broken pattern across the broad length of beach, his mind still fighting with the image of the trooper who had been killed seconds before. As he ran, despite his congestion of thought and emotion, he saw the force was making for a section of covering at the upper edge of the beach, a hollow formed of backwashed sand structure and rock outcropping. He knew it would be a position of self entrapment. He began to signal as he ran, directing the men to a point farther west along the foot of the rise.

A machine gun emplacement far above was scattering its fire across the beach at the running men. The troop leader stopped briefly, looking up. A lower machine gun position had stopped firing. He raised his Sten gun and opened a steady stream of fire at the upper German emplacement, shouting steadily as he looked up, and saw the men were being redirected to the points of cover farther to the west. His gun stopped firing and he began to run toward the high point, releasing the spent clip of the Sten and fitting a new one into place. He slapped the clip's end to be sure it was properly housed, then continued his broken run up the beach. He felt himself thrown sideward as he moved the final few feet, and lunged forward into the cover of a boulder some distance out from the upper edge of the open beach. He then began to fire again up along the slope toward the German shore emplacement. When he stopped briefly to look back, he saw the figure of one of the men of his platoon, crumpled and still, midway up from where they had touched down. He then became conscious of having been thoroughly soaked in falling as he jumped from the landing craft. He raised his hand to his left shoulder and felt the warmth of his wet battledress. As his hand came away he realized he had been hit. His hand was bright with the color of his own bleeding. He did not understand or remember having been hit, and thought to smile within himself at the strangeness of feeling no pain.

A sudden line of small eruptions along the ground close to where he lay roused him. He turned and looked up along the hills over the beach, then back toward the landing site. The other craft had touched down now and men were running. His vision blurred again and he shut his eyes tightly, then opened them. Men were still running and a pattern of smoke was rising out on the water above the motor launch. The launch had stopped, drifting easily back of the low surf, all its guns firing almost steadily. One of the running men had stopped by the figure that had fallen earlier. The man knelt briefly beside the figure, then rose and moved the remainder of the way to the cover of the upper part of the beach at a walking pace, looking back casually and raising an arm in signal to the others following beside him up from the water line.

The sixth landing craft nosed into the beach as others were backing off. The Germans were concentrating their fire on the landing craft now, and looking up, the walking figure, who was a captain and a company commander, assured himself the men were taking positions of cover from which they would be able to be organized into assault units to move up on the gun battery. He smiled to himself, knowing the meaninglessness of planning and assault. From the firepower being directed onto the beach, he knew there were two, or possibly three companies of riflemen up along the heights, in addition to the machine gun units. But yet, he thought, with the Bren gunners in the assault craft and the cover fire from the launch, we can push up along the rises.

Yes, he said to himself, push up along the rises... and then what?

The ramp of the sixth craft had not yet been lowered. The naval lieutenant was either having mechanical difficulty with the equipment, or they were coming under heavy and direct fire from above.

The Commando captain then began to run in toward the cover of the rise. He called to the men in their positions of cover, signaling by hand as he moved. The men hesitated briefly then began to rise and follow him, running to the left, eastward from the point on the beach where the landing craft had touched down.

He had seen the lower machine gun emplacements stop firing moments earlier. There was now a gap in the German fire zone, a narrow area in the stretch of broken rises where gunfire could not be placed from the upper positions. In running now, he was crossing into a line of fire, but he continued moving steadily, breaking the pattern of his movement. He stopped, kneeled and turned to see others moving up behind him. He then looked back toward the landing craft. The naval gunners had apparently seen this unit movement. Someone on board one of the craft had realized what the captain was attempting, and the full force of the cover fire was now directed onto the German positions commanding the lines of fire down toward where the captain and the men of his hastily organized unit were moving.

In a heavy rush forward and then up, slowing as

the loose gravel slipped backward beneath their boots, the men crossed the final open ground to the positions in the crossfire gap. The captain then signaled four men higher toward the silent machine gun emplacement.

Looking higher along the headland, he could see the concrete structures of the battery and its adjacent buildings. He motioned two teams of Bren gunners, indicating points of cover from which they could place the battery housings under direct fire. The sounds of gunfire from above slackened briefly, then rose in response to the Bren gunners opening bursts.

The Commando unit now drew heavy fire as the remainder of the men moved up from the beach. Another officer, leading a second unit, passed through the first occupied position, crossing eastward and working into a higher point of ground. Suddenly the firing broke off to the arhythmic patter of sporadic small arms. Looking down, the men saw that the landing craft had moved back from the beach. The captain noted that the sixth craft had lowered its ramp and the men aboard it had effected their landing. Two figures lay still at the water's edge. The L.C.P.s had backed beyond the low surf and were moving east, parallel to the shoreline. With the motor launch as escort, the craft were moving beyond range of the German gunners along the hill.

Away to the west, the sounds of distant gunfire began and the men knew the inner flank assaults had begun. The sudden knowledge that they were not merely an isolated unit fighting a meaningless independent skirmish had an uplifting effect on the entire unit. Under their officers' directions, the units dug into their positions along the rise and began a harassing fire up along the hillside that would immobilize the Berneval battery for hours.

At the point along the shore identified as "Yellow II" Beach, a single craft, L.C.P. (L) 15, landed twenty men of Number 3 Commando. They were about one mile west of the coastal point where the units had dug in above "Yellow I." The senior officer of the men put ashore was Major Peter Young. The naval lieutenant, H.T. Buckee, had brought them in unobserved. The men led by Major Young moved up from the beach to a narrow gully which gave access from this point of the beach. Lieutenant Buckee kept the landing craft beached, its guns poised to provide cover fire.

As Major Young and his unit moved inland, they heard the thin sounds of gunfire to the east and realized that men had landed and were fighting on "Yellow I" Beach. Checking the map that had been detailed from air photographs taken as recently as the day before, Major Young determined his unit's position and realized they were a short distance beneath the west flank of the gun battery that was the operational objective of this landing force. He held a hasty conference with two junior officers, then organized the party into small raiding units. Utilizing a series of leap-frog movements, the men moved up into the narrow depression toward the point above the village of Berneval-le-Grand where the 6-inch guns were emplaced. They came to within two hundred yards of the battery without being observed, then took cover and reorganized.

They could hear the fire beyond the hill on which the coastal battery was emplaced. Away to the south below them they saw a road and beyond that, the cluster of buildings of the village of Berneval-le-Grand. An unpaved side road led past the position they now occupied and rose toward the battery compound.

The force then spread across the broken patch of country with each man of the unit taking cover but retaining an open field of fire on one or another portion of the battery. Major Young knew their assignment had been to neutralize the battery. Now his best hope was to keep the guns from firing. The men were instructed to count their ammunition supply, and, unless attacked by an assault force of the enemy, to spread their use of ammunition over as long a period as possible. The men looked at one another, knowing the decision their commander had made would in all probability lead to their eventually being overwhelmed—if the enemy commander was a patient man.

"Nothing to be saved for a rearguard action, sir?" one of the men asked, smiling wryly.

"Let's live that long," one of the officers said. The final group separated, and on command, the men opened fire. It was by now 0510 hours.

The units dug in along the slope at "Yellow I" Beach heard the outbreak of gunfire beyond the battery and at first thought it to be the opening of an assault by additional enemy forces. But the closer

German firing broke off temporarily. The officers took the opportunity to move to points of observation, then ordered the Bren gunners to open fire up toward the battery. They knew before the firing began, now that they had proper observation, that they were out of range, and the firing would be ineffective. But the assault fire continued, and it brought a rush of gunfire from the German positions above.

The Commandos broke off their salvos, and the enemy firing once more slowed, then stopped.

The men of the "Yellow II" force took cover in their improvised positions and listened to the distant small arms fire beyond the headland. It would be almost a full hour before they would use their guns again.

Major Young's unit maintained the pattern of sporadic sniping at the battery, seeing little movement among the crews servicing the big guns. But the measure for them of the success of what they were doing was the continued silence of the 6-inch guns. Retaining a position from which he could observe the road that passed through Berneval-le-Grand, Major Young observed the movement of several vehicles that appeared to be troop carriers, moving north toward the coast. He knew the Germans were moving up reinforcements and alerted some of the men for a rearguard action in the event the new forces should come up along the road near which they were emplaced. He weighed carefully the option of abandoning the position from which they were sniping at the battery, not sure if a retrograde movement would serve his men any useful purpose. He did not know for sure whether the L.C.P. was still waiting on the beach. He decided the naval officer had likely withdrawn, and their own retreat would be rendered meaningless. His option was now to continue harrassing the battery until they were out of ammunition, and then surrender, or to organize for a strong, brief fight in attempting to storm the big guns.

The time factor was the significant element, he thought, and realized the larger purpose of the raid would best be served by continuing the sniping for as long as possible.

The movement of the troop carriers below continued along the road, still in the direction of the coast. The Major moved carefully from his command post to instruct the repositioning of his troops so that about half the force would be covering the access road. If the Germans were coming up here, they would be met by an ambush if not full-size, then at least full firepower.

They continued sniping, watching the road below, and waiting for the arrival of the reinforcements. The firing they had heard earlier, along the north side of the headland, had ceased. But the big guns had still not begun to fire.

High above them, the fighter cover had arrived, and looking west toward the main beaches of Dieppe the men could see that the assault of the center had begun. The Major hoped the rest of the raid would not become a battle of attrition such as this action was. He wondered about the fate of the remaining craft of Number 3 Commando, and of Lieutenant Colonel Durnford-Slater. Few enough, if any, of the remainder of the force had landed on the "Yellow" beaches, and without communications equipment, there was no way of calling for support fire from the naval guns. The destroyers were largely concentrated about the main beaches of Dieppe, at any rate, and he knew that so long as the coastal battery above did not begin to fire, the commanders in the headquarters ship would assume Number 3 Commando had achieved its objective.

Well, he thought, we are doing just that, just twenty of us. Yes, and however many of them are beyond the hill. If any of them are left.

The men beyond the hill, above "Yellow I" Beach, kept to their cover. The troop leader, dug in now above the lower command post, had become conscious of the pain of his wound. He had applied dressings from the medical pack he carried, but the bleeding had not stopped. He raised his head slowly, moving in an effort to ease the painfully cramped position of his left shoulder. In the movement, he saw the silhouette of men moving across the uppermost level of the rise. He heard his officer's voice almost at the same instant.

"Prepare to fire," the officer's voice called evenly. "They are coming down at us."

The officer had expected the downhill attack from the moment the German guns had stopped. He knew they had grouped for an assault, and he had been watching the crest of the hill. Now, as his voice trailed off, one of the German machine gun emplacements began to fire. The return fire rose instantly, and watching the open ground above, he saw the first of the Germans moving down. He raised his Sten gun and fired. He saw the man fall, thrown backward against the slope. The fallen German slid a short distance along the slope, and then others were moving down in back of him. The fire intensified, supported by increased machine gun fire from above. The Commando troops rose from their positions and rushed forward, but their impetus was stopped almost at once and they began to fall back, down the rise toward the beach. The Bren gunners lowered their elevation and began to fire at the oncoming Germans. The attack was slowed briefly, but the men of Number 3 Commando had been pushed back. There were far fewer guns returning fire up the slope now. One of the Bren gunners left his weapon behind as he moved out of his position and retreated down toward the head of the beach.

The Commando officer knew the men were running out of ammunition, but the German assault had been stopped. They were regrouping, he knew, and it would be only a matter of time before a second rush.

Silence fell once more over the north slope.

The men of Major Young's unit had heard the heavy but short-lived fire fight. His own rear guard ambush party had not observed any movement, and he realized that the reinforcements had been moved up for a rush on the Commando unit at "Yellow I"

Beach. He tried to decide whether the fight beyond the hill was over. He was still contemplating whether or not to rush the hilltop as a diversionary move, when the distant machine gunners opened up once more.

There had been a very short pause for the regrouping by the Germans. The second rush downhill came within minutes. The Commando force moved farther back and fell to cover. The officer commanding the British unit called for a cessation of firing, looked about him slowly, and moved out from his place of cover. He had raised his hands, and as he stepped clear, threw his weapon out to the side. Looking about him as he stepped forward toward the advancing Germans, he saw unmoving figures crouched under the scooped out seawall at the head of the beach. He stepped past the troop leader, whose eyes met his in the instant. He saw the man's shoulder and nodded.

"Well, lad," he said, "perhaps we'll have that properly seen to now."

The men on "Yellow I" Beach came out of their places of concealment and stood motionless. The firing had stopped all along the hillside. The officer looked at his wrist watch as a German came forward to formally accept his surrender. It was 1000 hours. They had kept the Berneval guns silent for close to five hours.

By final count, eighty two commandos surrendered on "Yellow I" Beach. Thirty eight of their number had been killed in the assault and following battle.

As the second silence ended, Major Young ordered his men to open in rapid fire on the battery. He then ran forward to the position of his point gunners and began to order the men to fall back. They were by now almost out of ammunition, and having still not come under enemy fire, he decided to try to get back to the beach. The force broke off their sniping and fell back, moving down along the road and back into the cover of the depression that led back to the shoreline. When they cleared the final section of elevated chalk cliffside and had a view of the beach, they saw the landing craft still sitting at the water's edge. The navy had waited. The full complement of twenty commandos raced down and across the open stretch of beach to the water. As the L.C.P. (L) 15 raised her forward ramp and moved out from the beach, Major Young noted that the Berneval battery had still not fired any of its 6-inch guns.

For their contributions to the action against the battery at Berneval, Major Young and Naval Lieutenant Buckee were both awarded the Distinguished Service Order.

9

The communications units on board the command headquarters ship off the beaches of Dieppe had been able to establish no contact at all with Number 3 Commando. Repeated calls to the signals group at "Yellow I" and "Yellow II" Beaches went unanswered, and naval escort craft were ordered to steam to the east and investigate.

The report on Major Young's small raiding party at "Yellow II" did not reach the Calpe until some time later. By then, General Roberts' greater concern had become the fate of the Royal Regiment of Canada, who were going into "Blue" Beach at the small resort village of Puys, between Dieppe and the still silent Berneval. The air strikes over Puys and the naval shelling had been observed at the two mile distance from where Calpe stood hove-to. But all signal calls had been interrupted by the heavy wireless traffic of inter-unit communications along the beaches, and none of the early messages from the destroyer Garth, whose operators were to provide links to Calpe, were received by the headquarters ship. The first message that did get through, in fact, was not received until after 0700. It read, ominously, "From Blue Beach: Is there any possible chance of getting us off?"

This cryptic message brought the concerned commanders to the awareness that whatever their conjectures had been about the Puys landings up to that moment, based on fragmentary messages and the visit to the Calpe a short time earlier by the Senior Officer of Blue Beach Landings, their prior information had all been misleading. General Roberts had, in fact, been of the impression that the Royals had not been landed at all, and had issued a signal for them to be redirected to land in support of the Essex Scottish on the main beaches at Dieppe, where the men of command were well aware of an already deteriorating situation in the main assault.

The sobered commanders then ordered a motor launch to provide close support for landing craft to approach the shores at Blue Beach and effect a withdrawal. It was already too late for the Royal Regiment of Canada, the attached units of the Canadian Black Watch, and the artillery crews and engineers.

It is said that no military operation is more difficult than the precise landing of troops in a night assault. The potential hazards implied in a military plan's success being contingent on the precision of such operations, with the added factor of reliance on the element of surprise, runs the operation up against odds that are almost insurmountable even at the level of conjecture. These same combinations, nonetheless, were the foundation of the "Blue" Beach assault at Puys. The additional factor of understandably incomplete knowledge of enemy defenses at the point of assault can add only further to the number of elements that, barring the perfection of precision, surprise, and extraordinary good fortune, comprise the makings of a disaster.

Good fortune abandoned the raiders of Dieppe in the hours before light, on the waters off Berneval, in Number 3 Commando's encounter with the German convoy. The other elements on which reliance can hardly ever be placed, came in rapid succession shortly thereafter. They began when the Royal Regiment of Canada were lowered in their landing craft from the decks of the landing ships Queen Emma and Princess Astrid, along with the Black Watch detachment from the Duke of Wellington.

One group of the assaulting craft formed up under a motor gunboat which had assumed a wrong position among the craft. It was wrongly taken to be the escort ship that would lead them into the beach. When this error was set right, valuable time had elapsed and the Landing Officers were obliged to approach the beaches at greater speeds than had been planned. Two mechanized landing craft, larger and more heavily armed than the ship-lowered assault craft, and each carrying one hundred men, were unable to match the speed of the smaller craft. They ultimately landed as a second wave, and one of these, in fact, developed engine trouble on the run into the beach and did not touch down until much later, a point of ironic good fortune, since the men in this L.C.M. were virtually the only troops of the Royal Regiment of Canada to return to England with the withdrawing forces after the raid.

The first wave of the Royals approached "Blue"

Beach twenty minutes late, at 0510 hours. The morning light had already come and, in an effort to counteract this difficulty, air controllers had requested a smoke screen be laid across the assault point. The onshore wind carried the smoke before the assault force and had little effect in concealing their approaches to the beach. The Germans, alerted by the earlier actions, were waiting for them.

Gunfire from the shore installations began when the first wave of craft were approximately a hundred yards from the beach. Still counting on the element of surprise, the sudden gunfire completely baffled the approaching force. But the landing craft continued their approach, escort craft now returning fire at the beach. The men in the craft, cool and controlled despite the sudden realization that the Germans were alert to their assault, moved to the forward sections of the craft, poised for the moment of touch-down and the lowering of the bow ramps.

As the L.C.P.s moved in and grounded against the shoreline, the ramps were lowered on signal, and the full force of the German gunnery suddenly came to bear on the exposed landing craft. Heavy casualties immediately began to mount. Major G. P. Schofield, the senior Royals officer in the first wave, was wounded during these opening moments. There were others wounded, and a large number of the troops were killed as they moved to strike the beach. The momentum of the assault continued under the fire and those who were not killed or badly wounded struck the shore and moved quickly across and up to the head of the beach, taking cover under a high stone sea wall. Looking back, the men who had reached the cover of the sea wall saw at once that more men than those who had reached cover lay dead or wounded in groups along the beach. Under the very heavy German fire, the landing craft had backed away from the beach and out of range.

More smoke was laid over the assault point and fighters of the air cover came in low, trying to place cannon fire among the German gun positions. Adding to the heavy machine gun fire, German mortars were now dropping with great accuracy along the beach.

Captain G. A. Browne, who was the Forward Artillery Observer with the assaulting force, landed with the second wave of L.C.P.s. He remembered the Royals in his armored landing craft as steady and cool, despite the approach being made under fire. This wave did not, in fact, know that other troops had gone in before them. It was almost light, and flares from the shore and the flashes of bombs were illuminating the interior of the A.L.C. He remembered afterward the even-toned voice of the officer seated beside him, Captain W. B. Thomson, steadying the men in the craft. His voice at times was drowned in the crackle of small arms fire passing overhead. From the instant of touchdown shells were striking the landing craft and... "here there was a not unnatural split-second hesitation in the bow in leaping out onto the beach. But only a split second. The troops got out onto the beach and across to the wall and under the cliff."

The second wave accomplished little more than add to the massing number of men sheltering under the sea wall, and to the numbers of the dead along the open beach.

"In five minutes," Captain Browne remembered, "they were changed from an assaulting Battalion on the offensive to something less than two companies on the defensive being hammered by fire which they could not locate."

A third wave of assault troops, with no signal received to countermand their action, also came ashore. With no information on the situation on the beach at Puys available, Captain R.C. Hicks and the naval flotilla officer made the decision to touch down. These were the craft lowered from the Duke of Wellington carrying the detachment of the Black Watch. At Hicks' order, they were put ashore under a cliff to the west of the sea wall, where most of the survivors of the earlier landings were now taking cover. The third landing was a repetition of the two earlier ones.

The air support continued. The fighters dove time and again, using their cannon to strike the German emplacements, and provided certain brief moments of relief from the relentless pounding the beach was taking.

The German positions were concentrated on the east cliff, with a complete command of the narrow beach. Along the cliff, almost directly overlooking the beach, a stone residence stood with what had appeared in aerial photographs to be a garden building alongside. This smaller building proved to be a concrete machine gun emplacement that effected a total field of fire command over the western section of the beach. At the head of the beach, covering the sea wall, barbed wire structures sealed the beach from access inland. The cliff dropped almost vertically, below the concrete pill box, to a long section of seawall to the east that virtually sealed the graveled beach at the waterline. On this beach, from which the only access was totally dominated by the concrete machine gun emplacement beside the stone house, the remnant of a force of more than six hundred men was trapped.

Captain Browne, who had the only wireless equipment in working order on the beach, was in contact with the destroyer Garth. The Garth received the messages concerning the wounded and dead along the beach, along with messages of the force being held up beneath the eastern seawall. These messages were retransmitted to the Calpe. But none of the messages reached Calpe until the alarming request of permission and advisability to be withdrawn. Whether attempts to withdraw the troops earlier could have been more effective, raises doubt. The German fire was such that approaching craft came under direct small arms and mortar fire. The exposed portions of the beach, which the troops would have had to cross, were even clearer targets.

The absence of good fortune, nonetheless, compounded the situation, extending as it did into the almost total lack of radio communication between the field commanders on the beach and the force commanders in Calpe.

Lieutenant Colonel Catto, commander of the Royals, did manage to lead a small force inland from the Puys beaches. Anticipating the likelihood of barbed wire along the sea wall, he had had Bangalore torpedoes brought ashore as part of the unit's armament. From the foot of the western sea wall, men climbed along the open stonework and set several of the explosive devices. The "torpedoes" were detonated, and with the Lieutenant Colonel leading, a party of men scrambled through the opening. But German gunfire was quickly concentrated on the opening. Only about twenty men made it through the wire, having to cut their way in places despite the detonated Bangalore torpedoes. After this first group, the German gunners sealed the opening, and no more men made it through. A good number, however, were either killed or wounded in the attempt.

The remainder of the Royals and the Black Watch held to their cover under the sea wall, unable to use their weapons because of the vertical stonework which, while it offered protection, obstructed totally any possible field of fire against the German positions above and back of them.

It is of significance to note that the defense at Puys comprised only two platoons, one of the German army, the second of Luftwaffe and technical personnel. Nor do German documents searched after the war indicate that this small garrison was reinforced during the action. The machine gun bunker, with mortars squads and a troop of howitzers, conducted the entire German defense.

Lieutenant Colonel Catto and his small party worked their way up the west side of the cliff, stopping frequently to return fire at the machine gunners who had them under observation. During the climb several men were wounded, but the force remained together and successfully scaling the cliff, they attacked and cleared a small house in from the edge of the promontory. They took cover for a time in a second building, which they found to be unoccupied. Then, hearing no sign of change or slackening in the incessant German gunfire down at the beach, Lieutenant Colonel Catto led the men in an southward march, clearing the area of the defense. His intent was to move west, remaining clear of the village of Puys, and attempt to join forces with the Essex Scottish, who had by this time landed in Dieppe, and whose operational plan, he knew, was to occupy the eastern perimeter of the town. But the Essex Scottish had never gotten off the beaches.

The Lieutenant Colonel's party ultimately took cover in a wooded area. Scouting attempts proved futile. They remained in their position of hiding until well into the afternoon, long after the operation had ended. Some time after 1600 hours, the party surrendered to German troops.

10

Of the two mechanized landing craft that made the final assault at Puys, one developed engine trouble and did not reach the beach until long after the entire initial assault force had landed. They had approached the beach under heavy shelling and small arms fire, and minutes before the craft touched down, there were already numerous casualties on board.

The Canadian correspondent Ross Munro was in this craft, and his report tells of the initial disbelief of the Canadians' first view of the beach after the ramp was lowered. Looking out beneath the pall of smoke that hung over the beach and seeing the open ground literally covered by the forms of men in battle dress, the Royals and those of the Black Watch on board began to fire at the emplacement along the cliff even before the ramp had finished lowering.

An officer positioned right next to the correspondent was struck by German gunfire as he fired his Sten gun. The battle on the beach had penetrated the landing craft. The storm of firing at the bow of the craft formed a solid curtain through which no troops could penetrate. The naval officer commanding the mechanized landing craft ordered the ramp raised and maneuvered the craft free of the shore. The L.C.M. then moved offshore in search of one of the larger ships with hospital installations in which to transfer the wounded.

This was the beginning of the withdrawal effort from Puys. It was almost the only one that met with any success.

Once withdrawal orders from the headquarters ship were relayed, the landing craft were organized in an effort to bring the troops off. With the motor launch escort, the craft which had been hovering out of range of the German howitzers approached the shoreline. But in the face of the German artillery and machine gun fire, no systematic evacuation could be organized. The troops in cover against the sea wall would have had to cross the beach to the water line, again coming under the German fire. With air support, the movement to the beach was initiated. The destroyer offshore set up a barrage of its 4-inch guns. The motor launch made broadside attacks running parallel to the beach, but took numerous direct hits and was heavily raked by machine gun fire. A near landing was made close to the west beach by several craft, but firing from above drove them back. The effort was repeated. The landing craft were severely damaged and their naval crews suffered many casualties. During the hours of repeated effort to bring landing craft into shore to evacuate the Royals, only one craft actually succeeded in landing. L.C.A. 209, commanded by Lieutenant N.E.B. Ramsay, R.N.V.R., approached the western part of the beach, lowering its ramp even before touching down and riding into a point of grounding.

Many soldiers, seeing the craft approaching the

beach, dashed from their cover beneath the foot of the sea wall and rushed across the beach. Many were hit as they ran, but most managed to reach the craft. It was by now under very heavy enemy fire. The Royals rushed aboard, throwing themselves into the craft, then falling to cover. The L.C.A. took several direct hits while it was beached. As it withdrew from shore, its ramp still partly lowered, its hull pierced by howitzer fire and loaded with troops beyond its capacity, it capsized not far from shore. Lieutenant Ramsay was among those who died then.

Several men clung to the exposed L.C.A.'s keel and two landing craft moved in again under the heavy crossfire, drew alongside the overturned L.C.A., and managed to rescue several of the men. The crew of the craft, however, suffered the loss of two of their number.

On shore, the remnant of the Royal Regiment and the Black Watch remained huddled in the cover of the high sea wall. And waited.

The Senior Officer, Blue Beach Landings returned from the Calpe and personally commanded another re-embarkation effort. Despite covering fire from escort craft offshore and the repeated strikes by protective fighter aircraft, the German gunfire resumed with such intensity that, beyond a rapid reconnaisance along the beach, no craft was able to approach closely enough to even attempt a landing.

The Senior Officer's signal, logged in the headquarters ship after 1100 hours stated: "Could not see position Blue Beach owing to fog and heavy fire from cliffs and White House. Nobody evacuated."

Standing offshore and hearing gunfire which falsely assured them that the Royals were still fighting, one more attempt was made to bring the men away. Four landing craft from the ship Princess Astrid moved in under smoke without escort craft. The naval officer commanding later reported heavy fire from shore. His signal ended, "there was no sign of life on the beach."

One landing craft was destroyed in the attempt.

Records would suggest that the final efforts to evacuate the Royals and Black Watch were in vain. The firing heard all through the late morning was probably German artillery directed at the offshore naval force. At 0835 hours, a report to the German 571st Infantry Regiment Headquarters and transmitted to the enemy's divisional command, stated: "Puys firmly in our hands; enemy has lost about five hundred men prisoners and dead."

A later analysis of figures indicated that of almost seven hundred men put ashore, fewer than one hundred were re-embarked, and most of these were accounted for in the mechanized landing craft that withdrew from the beach at the end of the assault without ever landing its troops. The force suffered almost six hundred casualties, including 240 dead, some of which were fatalities from wounds sustained in the raid, while prisoners of war.

The extent to which the failure of the assault at Puys may have compromised the major landings on the beaches of Dieppe cannot be minimized. The failure to secure the east headland provided the Germans complete command of artillery sites over the landing areas at Dieppe's eastern beaches.

It also illustrated the critical importance of totally dependable communications networks in combined operations of a multi-faceted nature. The inability to synchronize signals perpetuated a second and third-wave of assault craft being directed into an attack, which, as it was being mounted, had not the remotest chance of developing, let alone succeeding. It also brought about tragic delays in the transmission of command permission to commence re-embarkation efforts. The losses of time and the losses of life which resulted cannot be clearly calculated, but the consequences they precipitated cannot be ignored.

11

When one stands beside the bank of the River Scie as it flows into the English Channel at Pourville, the dominant view is of the heights to the east of the village. The beach here is long and open, a broad expanse of fine gravel, slanting at a gradual incline up away from the water's edge to the foot of a steeply rising series of chalk cliffs. In the valley formed by the dropping away of these cliffs toward the river basin, the village clusters about the river mouth. One major bridge crosses the Scie, carrying the coastal road east to Dieppe. After the morning of 19 August, 1942, the bridge would be remembered by the South Saskatchewan Regiment and the Cameron Highlanders of Canada as "Meritt's Bridge."

West of the village and the river mouth, the chalk cliffs rise again from the head of the beach, an uninterrupted palisade that stretches west along the coast beyond the observer's line of sight.

It was the eastern ridge of the Scie valley, which provided a natural command over the village and the coastline below, that, as much as the German force that occupied it, was the major adversary confronting the Canadian forces put ashore on that morning of 19 August.

Code named "Green" Beach, Pourville was the assault objective of the first wave of troops, the

South Saskatchewans. The eastern ridge had to be taken so that the Cameron Highlanders could link up with the tanks of the Calgary Regiment and the Royal Hamilton Light Infantry in their drive south from the beachhead at Dieppe, and then press inland to raid the aerodrome at St. Aubin. The ridge also served as the site of a radar station. The station was a major objective of the "Green" Beach assault force.

Beyond the objectives of the Dieppe operation, there were certain residual benefits that Combined Operations hoped would be achieved. There were the coastal batteries of Berneval and Varengeville, whose long range guns had long been a hazard to Allied channel shipping lanes. The radar station, as well as the batteries, if destroyed, could, in certain quarters, almost reconcile the entire raid.

The transfer of the assault force to the landing craft took place exactly on schedule and, with the destroyer Albrighton standing offshore to provide artillery support when requested, the force moved toward "Green" Beach. The landing craft moved in under the cover of pre-dawn darkness and touched down within a minute or two of the planners' scheduled time of 0450 hours.

The German guns began to fire simultaneously with the touch-down, but the Saskatchewans landed in a single wave and moved in to their individual unit objectives, encountering few obstacles in the opening action. One craft, which did not reach the beach until two minutes after the major landing force, came under very strong enemy fire and the troops suffered heavy casualties as they were disembarked.

Moving into the beaches under the cover of darkness, the assault craft crews were unable to strike the precise landing points intended, which were astride the mouth of he river. Almost the entire battalion of South Saskatchewans landed on the Pourville beach west of the river. With the vital objectives located along the east headland and ridge, the forces committed to these targets, Companies "A" and "D," would have to strike into the village of Pourville, then cross the river by way of the exposed bridge.

The advantage that had been gained in the surprise landing before dawn was thereby eliminated. And with no pre-assault artillery barrage, the enemy positions were readily manned. The two companies would have to fight their way to their primary assault points, the positions from which their attacks along the ridge would begin.

Moving into the village from the beaches, three companies fanned out in raiding units to the south and east. Moving south, "C" Company, which was to clear and consolidate the high ground southwest of Pourville, scouted carefully through the southwest corner of the village, neutralizing one street after another. They did not run into the Germans until they were almost beyond the last buildings of the town. The initial German opposition was disorganized, and in short rapid firefights, numerous Germans were killed and prisoners taken. The point platoon moved forward, passing the last structures of the village, coming into a piece of open

DIEPPE

An Allied destroyer lays down a smoke screen through which troop carrying invasion barges head for the beach during the raid that has been called a rehearsal for D-Day.

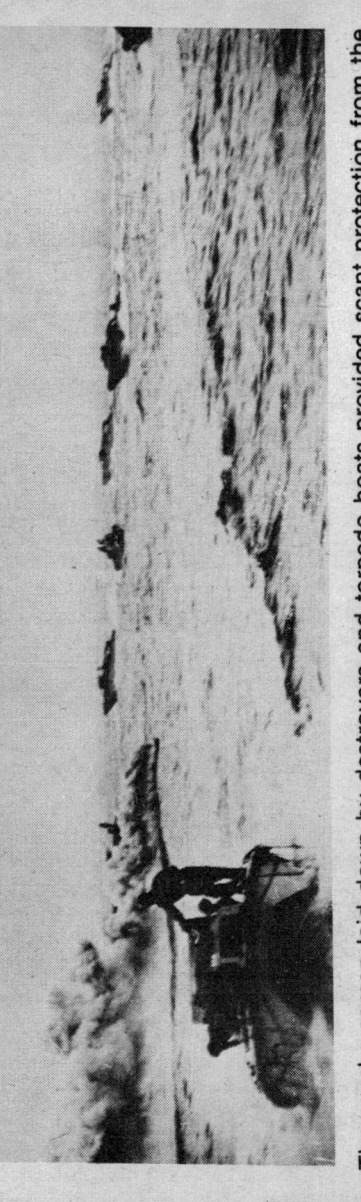

The smoke screen laid down by destroyers and torpedo boats provided scant protection from the German coastal guns. Hundreds of Allied troops died within minutes.

These Allied invaders didn't make it to the beach. Here, they are being hauled aboard a British destroyer after their assault craft was sunk by deadly German shellfire.

A wounded British commando is carried aboard a rescue ship by his comrades. A frontal attack against German machine guns cost the lives of thousands of men.

Returning according to schedule, with their faces still blackened, British and Canadian commandos wait to be evacuated after their historic raid on the French port.

British commandos take blindfolded German prisoners back to England for interrogation. Lessons learned at Dieppe were useful during Normandy invasion three years later.

The abortive Dieppe raid was truly a combined operation—British and Canadian commandos, American rangers, and a small contingent of Free French assault troops.

Wearing a German helmet, souvenir of the bloodiest raid of World War II, a British commando climbs on board a rescue ship for the 60-mile voyage back to England.

ground, and straight into the guns of a concealed unit of German infantry.

In the following minutes, the Canadians were stopped, then pushed back to points of cover. The platoon leader had been seriously wounded, and other casualties had considerably diminished the platoon's firepower.

Private W.A. Haggard took rapid command, recalling the platoon and organizing the men into one holding force under another Private, G.B. Berthelot. Haggard led the other half of the platoon out in an encircling maneuver to strike the German position from a flank. Private Berthelot had his men lay down a heavy covering fire while the others moved out. As Private Haggard brought the small flanking force down on the German position, Berthelot went forward, firing a Bren gun from a hand held position, drawing the German counter-fire while the other force completed the flanking move and overpowered the German position in sharp hand-to-hand fighting. The fight ended in a fierce exchange of close gunfire, and the Germans who had not been killed in the skirmish were marched down to the beach as prisoners.

Both Privates Haggard and Berthelot continued fighting through the action in Pourville and were subsequently awarded Distinguished Conduct Medals. Company "C" then continued its advance into the southwest high ground overlooking Pourville, routed out other minor German resistance, and dug in. Having assumed command of the objective, they reported their position to Lieutenant Colonel C.C.I. Merritt, the unit commander who had established his post at the head of Pourville Beach. The company maintained this high ground through the morning, sending out frequent patrols southwest of Pourville, and further consolidating its positions. After a time they were able to hear the rising sounds of small arms fire from static positions across the village as Companies "A" and "D" approached their assault positions facing the east headland.

Scouting units of the two eastward moving companies came on the approaches to the bridge from the west, through the streets of Pourville. They had encountered only sporadic fire until now, and the movement up from the beaches and through the village had been steady. At the bridge, the advance unit moved into open ground and became the immediate target for a sudden barrage of pre-registered mortar salvos, fired from positions to the east. The initial confrontation at the beginning of the bridge brought rapid changes in the movement of the force. Men ran out onto the bridge, taking cover where they could, then moving in sprints, firing their small automatic weapons toward the east end of the bridge as they did. The main bodies of the company units came up and attempted numbers of assaults beyond the bridge entrance. Small groups of men became pinned down along the few points of cover the bridge provided. Then the enemy mortar fire began to spread to other targets while still remaining concentrated on the approaches to the bridge. The units that had reached the bridge and moved out along it were forced to stop by the murderously accurate fire. Bodies of Canadian soldiers began to cover the bridge's roadway, and the movement of the skirmishers on the bridge making their way eastward slowed to a halt. The bridge had become totally dominated by the enemy fire from the east.

Some of the men had gotten across the bridge and established fire points from what cover they could find. Others, trapped along the span, gave cover fire to the new efforts to get the companys' forces across. Several more efforts were made to storm the bridge, but all were stopped by the German gunfire.

Lieutenant-Colonel Merritt had left his command post and approached a point of observation back of the bridge. He found the two companys of Saskatchewans consolidated before the bridge, the small units along the bridge span held in static exchanges of gunfire with the enemy. Rapidly organizing a small skirmish force behind him, the Lieutenant Colonel moved boldly forward and walked evenly out onto the western entrance of the bridge. He stopped, turned, and began calling to the men of Companys "A" and "D," then continued his steady movement forward, the enemy gunfire incessant all along the bridge. Men then began to move forward, and new units assaulted the bridge approach.

Merritt removed his helmet and began waving the men forward, continuing across the bridge to the far side, having miraculously avoided the heavy German gunfire. His incredible march across the bridge injected a new momentum to the assault. He remained on the bridge, in exposed positions, cheering the men on, returning and leading several parties of troops across, calling encouragement to others who had descended to the lowland beneath the bridge and forded the narrow river.

The assault reached the eastern end of the bridge with Lieutenant Colonel Merritt at its head. They were gradually reinforced by troops of the Cameron Highlanders, who had been landed in the second wave at "Green" Beach.

Maintaining the forward thrust, the Canadians made a repeated series of rushing assaults along the beginnings of the headland, Merritt leading several of the attacks. They reached and fought their way into numerous concrete gun emplacements that had been commanding the bridge and the eastern perimeter of the village. The forces consolidated east of the bridge, then struck out at their specific objectives. By 0700, after almost two hours of intensive combat at close quarters, the Saskatchewans had reached a subheadquarters office of the German 6th Company, 571st Regiment, along the headland. They had attacked and overrun several anti-tank gun positions, taken and destroyed a small field gun battery, and put out of commission several of the machine gun emplacements below the outer defenses of the radar station.

One advance force reached the radar station. Its outer defenses were heavily covered with barbed wire barricades and machine gun units. Without artillery support, the men were unable to capitalize on the successful penetration. South of the radar installation, which was at the summit of the east cliffs, a series of trench defenses fringed a field gun battery and a strategic position known as Quatre

Vents Farms. The defenses along this system were very heavy, and several thrusts against the machine gun outguards were forced back. One point scout unit, with Sergeant K.A. Williams among its number, reached the edge of the Quatre Vents position. They engaged the enemy defenders briefly, in a fight of short rushing movements and intense gunfire, and overcame a German unit, killing several enemy troops before being forced to withdraw.

During these headland skirmishes, Captain H.B. Carswell, the forward artillery observer, called numerous barrages from the Albrighton. Several salvos were fired by the destroyer's 4-inch guns, but the observer's inability to spot the fall of the shells and the lack of precise information on positions of his own advance forces rendered this effort to support the troops of little value.

During the rushing series of assaults against the east headland, the Cameron Highlanders of Canada were put ashore on "Green" Beach. The landing craft approached the beach, and under the sound of the German artillery fire and the shriek of shells exploding along the water in their path, the skirl of bagpipes sounded through the morning.

It was apparent, from the extent of defensive fire the oncoming craft were encountering, that the Saskatchewans had not broken through the Pourville defenses. They could see the fight raging along the hillside on their left. These were the initial skirmishers led by Lieutenant Colonel Merritt. But they could also see the artillery emplacements from which the shellfire directed against their beaching assault craft was coming. The craft moved in toward the beach, entering the area of the shelling. During the final run to the beach, none of the craft was hit.

The Camerons were landed directly at the river mouth, a smaller force on the east bank, and the main force on the west, above the village. Accompanied by the pipers, the advance forces east of the river rushed forward to dismantle the barbed wire barricades running parallel courses along this beach. The unit's commander, Lieutenant Colonel A. C. Gostling, was among the first ashore. He moved forward with the wire-cutting detail, signalling the others from the craft, and establishing contact with the other landing force through a signalman. He reached the first barricade as a German machine gunner commenced firing along the east beach.

The German emplacement was the single position along the low east headland the Saskatchewans had not overrun, and in its opening bursts of fire, the Cameron's commander was instantly killed. Other casualties were suffered as the troops worked their way up from the beach. The main force moved into the headland in support of the Saskatchewans, as ordered by Major A. T. Law, who had taken command on Lieutenant Colonel Gostling's death.

Pourville was by now under almost constant mortar fire from the commanding emplacements to the east above the village. The Saskatchewans were making their valiant but futile effort to break the German command of the field of fire. Major Law, who had landed with the Cameron forces west of the river Scie, led the assaulting force up off the beach and into the cover of the village. The Cameron forces under Major Law comprised almost three complete companies, less the broken platoons that had landed at the east end of the beach. It was well past 0600 hours by now, and knowing their battle order accounted for a maneuver inland to merge with the Calgary tanks coming from Dieppe, Major Law organized his force and struck inland through Pourville.

The original plan had been for the Camerons to advance inland along the east bank of the Scie, linking up with the tanks in the Bois de Vertu some three miles inland. They were then to assault the aerodrome adjacent to the covering forest. The Saskatchewans, in their preliminary assault had not cleared the east route, and since time, by now, was of essence, Major Law decided on an alternate route along the west bank. The Camerons moved out, following the main road south. It made rapid progress inland until coming under fire from the fortified emplacements of Quatre Vents Farms across the river. Major Law then ordered the force up off the road, and forward through the cover of a dense wood along the heights overlooking the river valley.

The troops picked their way through the densely wooded hillside, flanking scout parties moving ahead slowly, alert for German patrols now that they knew the Germans were aware of their presence. From maps, Major Law knew of a crossing over the Scie through the hamlet of Petit Appeville (Bas de Hautot). He moved the force south until they were about a mile and a half inland, then brought them down through the hillside until his forward scouts were overlooking the river crossing and the small village.

He joined the forward observation unit and began to glass the area. The crossing was unguarded but beyond the bridge he saw groupings of German soldiers stopped along the road. He also observed a force of infantry moving along the road on bicycles. But the Calgary tanks were not there.

Totally without information on either the enemy disposition, or, for that matter, the situation among the units landed on the main beaches at Dieppe, Major Law ordered the force to take cover and rest while he evaluated the situation. It had taken the force more than two hours to advance along the river to where it now was grouped. The hour was late, and Major Law had begun to have apprehensions as to the fate of the tanks, which had, in fact, never gotten beyond the promenade above the Dieppe beach.

He knew his force, operating alone, could never pursue the planned assault on the aerodrome. They carried no weapons heavier than Bren guns, their 3-inch mortars having been hit in Pourville. The plan had been contingent on the tanks covering fire over the Camerons' assault. Time was pressing, and efforts to establish communications with the coastal points came to no use. Seeking, nonetheless, to exploit the inland advance, Major Law decided to abandon the original battle order and, in its place, cross the river at Petit Appeville and attack the fortification at Quatre Vents Farms. He discussed a planned route down to the road with his junior officers, then dismissed the hastily drawn conference, the order for movement being for 0900 hours, just minutes ahead.

Advance parties descended from the hillside to the road north of the crossing point. As the main body of the force moved down, movement was heard north of the road. The Camerons took assault positions and fell to cover. Before anything came into sight, another force was spotted by the men closest to the crossing point, moving north along the opposite river bank. There was no possible concealment, and on order, the Camerons broke from cover and began firing, first at the moving force across the river, then organizing a hastily drawn ambush on a reconnaisance unit of engineers which had been moving down away from Pourville. The Camerons saw the Germans of both units hit in the fighting, which broke off rapidly with the withdrawal of the German forces.

Before they could regroup and assess the situation, they were hit from the south, this time by yet another German unit. The Camerons consolidated along the road and returned fire. Under cover of the forward German gunners, Major Law could see a detachment of field artillery being moved up. Horse-drawn defense guns, which were moved across the river through the fighting, took up positions converging on the crossing from the east.

From their positions two hundred yards north of the crossing, the Camerons then came under machine gun fire from above. The Germans had obviously covered the crossing from high ground. Sniper fire was added to the machine gunners as well as the force covering the field guns at the crossing.

Shortly after 0930 hours, Major Law ordered a withdrawal of the entire Camerons force. As the troops organized and began to draw back, fighting a rear guard action as they moved back up into the wooded hills, his signalmen rushed up to inform him that a message to the Saskatchewans had been monitored. It related to an intention to withdraw the forces, evacuating Pourville directly from "Green" Beach. The message had carried with it the order to transmit the retrograde instruction on to his unit. The Major wanted to know if a time of evacuation had been mentioned and was told 1000 hours, less than thirty minutes away.

Major Law signaled the Saskatchewans that his force was moving back, and the Camerons began their withdrawal. The German gunners moved up back of them, a running fight commencing which continued throughout the march. At one point the advance unit was joined by a platoon of the Saskatchewans who had been sent forward to make contact. The forces combined, fighting their way north past rapidly organizing German flanking units, and made their way into the streets of Pourville just before 1000 hours.

The original battle plan had called for the Pourville forces to be re-embarked through Dieppe. But with circumstances as they had developed through the morning of fighting, a hasty evacuation had been ordered directly from "Green" Beach. The time scheduled for the movement was 1100 hours,

110

and not 1000 hours as had been misunderstood in the message intercepted by the Camerons. The mistaken message had, in fact, likely saved Major Law's force, since subsequent records show that the running fight which engaged the Camerons in their movement north away from Petit Appeville was indeed against the advance units of a major attack being launched by the German 302nd Infantry Division.

Along the stretch of "Green" Beach, the German artillery and mortar had resumed full command from the east heights. In the southwest sector of Pourville, Company "C," which had made the first consolidated penetration of the landing, had begun to withdraw from their positions. This had been due to a misinterpretation of an order. They had actually been intended to establish a holding action from their commanding position. The German forces approaching the village from the south now encountered a rear guard action that was in reality a street-by-street battle fought by the Camerons and the South Saskatchewans as they moved back toward the beaches.

More than a dozen craft approached the beaches just before 1100 hours, including support vessels. The machine gun fire formed a virtual wall across the beach, and mortars and field gun shells broke the waters along the shoreline. The losses suffered by the troops retreating through the village was seriously compounded as the Canadians began to rush down along the beach when the landing craft touched down.

Fire support began to come in from the destroyers offshore, directed at the east headland. The sounds across the beach—mortars detonating, machine gun salvos, men calling out as they ran, firing behind them, other men falling—rose to a height where sound became indistinguishable. No orders could be given, no calls for help heard. Nothing... only deafening sound.

Commanding the rearguard in Pourville, Lieutenant Colonel Merritt and a small force held the advancing Germans back in a series of savagely fought close-in battles. Frequent hand-to-hand struggles took place as the men were gradually forced back, relinquishing ground to the Germans at almost literally arm's length.

The greatest number of casualties suffered by the Canadians were during these final minutes of battle.

Behind the rear guard, the Saskatchewans and Camerons retreated across the broad beach, running the gauntlet of German fire, and entering the shallow water where the landing craft and escort vessels awaited them. During the re-embarkation, four of the landing craft were destroyed by gunfire, and many of the withdrawing troops were wounded. But most of them got off the beach, support craft taking on survivors. Other men moved out to deeper water, swimming until they were picked up. Still others left the beach in small wooden craft they had scavenged in the last minutes along the shore. The nightmare of the beach pursued them into the water as the German gunners maintained the relentless barrage until they were out of range.

The rear guard fought back to the beach. Lieutenant Colonel Merritt and the others held the Germans above the low sea wall at the head of the gravel slope, still firing as the last of the withdrawing craft eased back from the shore. The rear guard unit was left behind, and the men in the landing craft continued firing back, lending what support they could to the men they had been forced to abandon.

Merritt was seen to be wounded, but despite this he continued fighting. From out on the water as they moved off, they watched him walk down to the waterline and help another wounded man back up along the gravel beach to the shelter of the sea wall, then resume firing at the Germans.

Merritt and his remaining force were able to hold out along the beach until they had expended almost their final rounds of ammunition, clinging to the hope of a last attempt by one of the naval craft to evacuate them. It never came. Merritt and his force finally surrendered, more than an hour after the last of the evacuees had left the beach of Pourville.

Lieutenant Colonel Merritt was later awarded the Victoria Cross.

12

The thousand year old seaport of Dieppe, whose first castle had been built by Charlemagne, had seen one of its native sons, Jean Parmentier, embark on Sixteenth Century voyages of discovery that resulted in his name being added to the list of history's illustrious navigators. Other adventurers sailed from Dieppe to the coasts of Africa, and in 1543, her seamen visited the bay that became New York Harbor. The port's origins are believed to stem from Norman adventurers, for whose sailing craft its *diep* or natural inlet formed an ideal anchorage. It was attacked by Philip Augustus in 1195, and plundered in 1339 by the English. The town was occupied by England from 1420 to 1435, and a siege launched by the First Earl of Shrewsbury in 1442 was relieved in a military expedition by the *dauphin*, who would later become Louis XI. The day of its deliverance from the siege was commemorated for centuries with religious festivals. One of Henry IV's great battles was fought in the neighboring village of Arques, now called Arques-la-Bataille.

The revocation of the edict of Nantes in 1685 brought great suffering to its citizenry, and less than ten years later the port was destroyed in a bombardment by the British and Dutch. It was later rebuilt but did not again prosper until the nineteenth century when the railway, built in 1848, stimulated its trade and activities as a modern port.

The fashionable socialites and royalty of late nineteenth century Europe followed a style set by Marie Caroline, Duchess of Berry, and Dieppe flourished as an internationally famed resort and watering place.

Occupied during the Franco-Prussian War, the port later became a fondly remembered staging point for U.S. troops in 1918. Its Gare Maritime saw the arrival, through the years between the wars, of innumerable cross channel steamers carrying passengers from the English port of Newhaven. In 1939 it became a hospital center for British forces of the B.E.F., which it remained until the fall of France in 1940.

Now, in the dark early hours of 19 August, 1942, it was a well fortified garrison within the assigned area of the German 302nd Infantry Division. To the German Armed Forces High Command, its proximity to the English coast across the channel had rendered it a key point in the coastal defense system.

Early in 1942, the German high command had evolved a strategic point of view which emphasized that, with Russia still fighting in the east, it was of the essence that all efforts be made to prevent the opening of a second front, or the possibility that "at critical moments the British might create difficulties." Adolf Hitler had issued specific directives on the defense of the French coast. Their implementation came to be known as the Atlantic Wall, a system of defenses designed to make a fortress of the Atlantic and Channel coasts.

Within Dieppe, the defensive fortifications were well along toward completion. Certain buildings adjacent to the beaches had been demolished, and even the famed Casino had been partially dismantled to facilitate the defensive capabilities of the new gun emplacements. On 8 August, the headquarters of the 302nd Infantry Division had ordered a state of "threatening danger" (*drohende gefahr*) for the ten nights from 10 August through 20 August because the moon and tides were favorable to the possibility of landings along the coast.

It was against this state of preparedness that the forces of the Dieppe operation launched their assaults at Berneval, Varengeville, Puys, Pourville at 0450 hours, 19 August, 1942. And now, thirty minutes later, the command group in the destroyer Calpe ordered the commencement of the frontal attack against the main beaches of Dieppe.

Four destroyers, including Calpe, opened an intensive artillery bombardment of the shoreline. The first wave of landing craft, carrying the Royal Hamilton Light Infantry and the Essex Scottish, were by now one mile from the shoreline. From above and back of them, five squadrons of R.A.F. Hurricanes roared in over the water and dove on the coastal points above the main beaches, their cannon firing steadily, thousands of shells pouring into the German coastal defenses. The Essex Scottish and the Hamiltons saw the final moments of the Hurricane's attack as their craft moved into the beach, the coastal points ahead of them erupting in a wall of orange flashes and deafening explosions under the repeated cannon fighter attacks.

But from that wall of destruction, machine gun fire had already begun to sweep the beaches and on out over the water. As the landing craft moved into the beach, the Germans had already found the range. Gunfire was striking the hulls of the landing craft as the ramps were lowered and the men began to strike the beach.

Timed to land as part of this first wave, three tank landing craft (L.C.T.s) carrying the first contingent of the Calgary Regiment's armor, were to have put nine Churchill tanks on the beach to support the first wave of infantry. The L.C.T.s approached the beach too far to the west and were some ten minutes late in landing. This was the first time the Churchill tanks would be used in battle. More significantly, it was the earliest test of tank landing craft in operation under actual combat conditions.

The Essex Scottish and the Hamiltons moved up from the shore and into the hastily reorganized gunfire of the German coastal emplacements. With no heavy guns supporting their move up the beach, they were quickly pinned down before they could break through the wire barricades along the beach. Under the cover fire of their own riflemen, the forces along the beach began struggling to cut their way through the wire and reach the sea wall. But the casualties had already begun to mount. Two of the landing craft, carrying units of the Hamilton's "D" company, were completely wrecked by German gunnery before they reached the beach. The others of the company, which had approached the extreme right flank of the beach directly beneath the west headland, were, according to the testimony of Hamilton officers, "completely wiped out" immediately after landing. By the time the tank landing craft approached the beach, much of the initial momentum of the assault had already begun to ebb.

Dawn had come, and the new morning had just begun.

The three tank landing craft of the first wave, "Flight I," approached the beach below where the infantrymen were fighting to break through the primary obstacles. L.C.T. 2 landed its three tanks near the east headland, experiencing some delay with mechanical malfunctions. The three Churchills finally rode down onto the beach and immediately began giving support fire over the troops. The craft withdrew from the beach, its officer intending to land an engineer detachment at a point farther west. Shellfire had damaged the ramp mechanism and the craft was unable to land again, the engineers never reaching shore. L.C.T. 1 put its tanks ashore along the west end of the beach, but was so severely shelled during the landing operation and directly afterward that it sank in the shallows close to shore. The third craft of "Flight I" offloaded its first tank in a deep shoreline depression. The Churchill was drowned on touchdown. The two other tanks were successfully landed, but the craft, under heavy fire from the moment of touch-down, was unable to withdraw from the beach and was thus lost.

The east beach, code named "Red," had been the target of the Essex Scottish. It had no natural features to provide cover for the landing forces and was dominated by gunfire from the headlands both east and west of Dieppe. It faced, as well, a concentration of German positions established in the buildings along the Promenade beyond the beach. Of the entire unit, only one group penetrated the town.

Under cover of the tanks' gunfire, Warrant Officer Cornelius Stapleton led an assault group through the wire barricade and up off the beach. Under constant gunfire, the men dashed across the promenade and into the entrances of buildings facing on the Boulevard de Verdun. A second group of Essex Scottish followed Stapleton's earlier force. Of nine men in the second group, only two reached the buildings to join Stapleton. The assault group took cover in the buildings, firing at snipers, holding to cover while Warrant Officer Stapleton sought a route through the streets so the force could strike through to the small harbor.

On "Red" Beach, the Hamiltons faced the partly demolished Casino. It stood at the west end of the Promenade and was flanked by numerous German gun emplacements. The Hamiltons had broken through the wire barricades in several places and begun making thrusts forward, rifle units reaching the low sea wall at the west end of the beach, taking cover, then moving out in strike forces, trying to reach the cover of the Casino building, which they could see was unoccupied save for some snipers.

The tanks behind them which had been landed began to provide covering fire while they moved up. Traction was difficult on the loose and slippery gravel of the beach and several of the Churchills "bellied," became immobilized, and never moved farther up along the western area of the beach.

The Hamilton assault squads began to overcome the sniper fire from the Casino and Bren gunners and several riflemen, rushing forward and throwing grenades, overpowered two gun emplacements alongside the building. A final thrust by a force led by Lance Sergeant G.A. Hickson of the Engineers finally bridged the open space across the Promenade. They entered the cover of the Casino and were quickly followed by a unit under the command of Captain A.C. Hill.

Along the rest of the beachfront, the larger part of the landing units were held in static gunfire exchange with the German emplacements. In the east, on the Essex Scottish beach, the Churchill tanks had begun to move up toward the Promenade.

Warrant Officer Stapleton of the Essex Scottish had, meanwhile, led a force into the inner streets of Dieppe. They worked from building to building, penetrating several buildings and rushing sniper positions, and finally made their way to the edges of the harbor area, north of the Gare Maritime. A strong force of German patrols was met here, and Stapleton and his men grouped at the edge of a building and began firing. They could see, beyond the Germans, the open waters of the small harbor, and many small ships and sailing craft tied in along the wharves. Beyond the harbor, in the *le Pollet* section, there was enemy gunfire being directed at the beach from windows of the higher buildings.

The small force under Stapleton continued their action, a number of the men being cut down by German fire, until almost 0800 hours, when they were rushed and driven back. The remnant of the attackers, with Stapleton still commanding, made their way back to the beach, where he reported to the Essex Scottish commander, Lieutenant Colonel F. K. Jasperson.

A German excavating crew had been employing machinery along the beach, prior to the raid, to deepen the depression before the sea wall. This had made the central sections of the wall impassable to the tanks. But at the eastern end of the beach, the wall was little more than two feet high, and at this point a number of the Calgary tanks crossed to the Promenade. They moved forward, their guns firing into the high buildings, drawing German fire away from the troops dug in along the beach, with the intent of penetrating the town. But a series of concrete roadblocks blocked the roads leading out of the Promenade. The roadblocks had been anticipated from examination of aerial photographs taken before the raid. These had been among the objectives of the engineer forces, who were to be moved in with infantry support, to demolish them with explosive charges. But many of the "sapper" units had not been landed, and others had suffered severe casualties. Despite several efforts to destroy the roadblocks, they were never breached. Most of the tanks that reached the Promenade ultimately withdrew to the beach before the action was ended.

In the Casino, up from "White" Beach, Captain Hill led a force of 14 Hamiltons through the depth of the building. Other troops were still clearing the snipers from deeper parts of the structure. The Casino spread across the depth of the Promenade, and Captain Hills' force was able to reach the Boulevard de Verdun completely under cover. The time was about 0600, and under the covering fire of Bren gunners raking the windows of the buildings across the road, Captain Hills' assault unit crossed the Boulevard, took cover in the open buildings, and broke into a theater. They rushed into the large hall, passing swiftly between rows of seats down to the corridors beside the stage entrances. Here they found exits that led onto the road beyond, and broke out into the town. The patrol became a rapid foraging expedition, seeking the enemy and engaging them, patrolling through several open streets in the interior of Dieppe.

On "Red" Beach, the Essex Scottish organized an attack across the sea wall, which was launched at about the time Captain Hills' Hamiltons were moving through the streets. The Essex Scottish attack moved out, rushing out from the cover of the wall and breaking across the Promenade toward the building that was clearly identified by its two high chimneys. This was the tobacco factory and was believed to be an explosives storehouse. The men of "D" Company, whose orders had included the destruction of the factory, reached within close enough range to fire rifle grenades into the building before being thrown back. The building soon began to burn fiercely and continued doing so throughout the hours of the raid.

The naval escort craft had, by this time, begun to move closer to shore, providing what support fire they could. A destroyer made a sweep along the beach and lay smoke to cover the onshore movements of the men. The air cover was heavy with R.A.F. fighters, but German aircraft began to break through the defensive screen, and bombs began to fall among the ships. The Essex Scottish assault was thrown back, but was soon remounted. The men reorganized and rushed forward a second time, their assault being met with heavy gunfire from a largely unseen enemy. They ultimately withdrew to the beach again, took up defensive positions, and returned enemy fire while efforts began to tend the wounded. Casualties were mounting steadily.

The second wave of Calgary tanks was landed about this time. The L.C.T.s moved into the beach and, under continued heavy fire, landed nine more Churchills. Only four succeeded in getting past the sea wall to the Promenade. Of the landing craft, one L.C.T. sank after withdrawing from the beach, and a second, L.C.T.5, was immobilized on the beach directly below the Casino. This craft succeeded in withdrawing from the beach and joined the support craft off shore. A further detachment of tanks arrived on the beach shortly afterward, numbering twelve more Churchills.

One of the craft also carried the Calgary Regimental headquarters unit. The headquarters craft touched shore and lowered its ramp. The first tank rushed forward and down the ramp, only to become lodged in the loose gravel at the water line. The crew quickly withdrew a few yards to clear the blockage of the ramp, and as it did so, German shellfire severed the ramp's cable. The next tank in position to unload was the command vehicle, that of Lieutenant Colonel Andrews, the Calgary's commanding officer. He was signaled to offload, the crew believing he could clear what depth of water remained between the ramp and the shoreline. The tank ran down the ramp and was almost entirely submerged in eight feet of water. Colonel Andrews and his crew climbed out of the tank's turret and jumped toward the shore. They were killed by gunfire at the water's edge.

The tanks from the remaining L.C.T.s all reached the beach and succeeded in getting up from the beach across the sea wall, but none penetrated the road blocks of the Promenade.

Lance Sergeant Hickson of the Hamiltons led a

second unit through the Casino. Under cover fire of one of the tanks which had reached the Promenade and had silenced machine gun emplacements along the west headland near the town's Castle, Hickson's 18 men crossed to a near building and engaged an infantry troop. There was heavy hand-to-hand fighting, but Hickson's unit finally overcame the German force and took over the building, establishing a gun position from which they fired at snipers and machine gun units for a long time.

Captain Hill and his men continued ranging through the streets of Dieppe until German forces organized and began to close in on them. They slowed before the increasingly accurate German gunfire, then pulled back and took cover in the theater building which they had first occupied. Other Hamilton forces were there and the combined units established a defensive position which they continued to hold until about 1000 hours. A heavy German assault party attacked, and they withdrew through the Casino to the beach.

Close to the shore line a naval craft of new design, actually a converted L.C.T. mounting several anti-aircraft guns and crews, added considerable support to the forces on the beach. When they were not firing overhead at attacking German aircraft, the gunners raked the targets beyond the beach—the gun emplacements in buildings along the Boulevard and the artillery batteries in the cliffs beyond the Castle.

The L.C.T., despite heavy enemy fire, remained close inshore all through the morning. One by one her gun crews were hit, and finally, after a particularly fierce artillery barrage, she sank in shallow water.

On the beach, as the casualties mounted, men began to construct more adequate shelter under the sea wall. Others moved from group to group, providing medical aid to the wounded. One of these was Honorary Captain J. W. Foote, Chaplain of the Royal Hamilton Light Infantry. He worked with medical aides in carrying wounded troops to the hastily organized field posts and moved from one section of the beach to another administering first aid and carrying supplies, constantly exposing himself to enemy gunfire in bringing aid to the wounded.

As the morning wore on, the battle from the beaches grew more static, a holding action somewhat supported by the tanks that succeeded in getting over the sea wall and onto the Promenade. Gunfire from both sides remained steady, and with the support of the offshore gunfire and the aerial sorties, the Essex Scottish and the Royal Hamilton Light Infantry established a solid, unmoving line of battle. They had not been able to bring that line higher than the sea wall below the Promenade, except for the raiding parties such as those of Warrant Officer Stapleton, Captain Hill, and Lance Sergeant Hickson. The only organized force that got beyond the beach was the tank group that reached the Promenade.

On board the Calpe, General Roberts attempted to control the situation on the strength of wireless reports that came in through the morning. The reports that reached Calpe of the actions on the beach were distorted, some were largely exaggerated, others were totally erroneous. The report that the Royal Regiment of Canada had not landed at Puys prompted the Commander to divert the force to the support of the Essex Scottish on "Red" Beach. This was because a report, retransmitted from the destroyer Fernie, stated: "Essex Scot across beaches and in houses."

This was a distortion of a series of retransmitted wireless reports which originally described Warrant Officer Stapleton's raiding force into the town. Reaching General Roberts in the form it did, it led the Commander to the assumption that the Essex Scottish had broken through the beach defenses.

In addition to the useless order committing the Royal Regiment of Canada to "Red" Beach at Dieppe, the order was issued to the floating reserve unit, Les Fusiliers Mont Royal, to go in at "Red" Beach.

At 0700 hours, the twenty six landing craft carrying Les Fusiliers Mont Royal organized under support naval craft and moved in toward the beach.

13

Lieutenant Colonel Dollard Ménard, the commanding officer of Les Fusiliers Mont Royal, was among the first men of his force to hit the beach. He had been in one of the lead craft approaching the shore line, watching the incoming German gunfire, noting with a grim recognition that the gunners were rapidly getting the range as small arms fire began to strike the craft. The final seconds before touchdown brought within him a rage at the confinement of the craft. Some of the men had already been wounded, and, as the assault vessel touched the shore, the sound of the German guns rose to a continuous roar. The ramp was lowered as the craft skidded against the gravel beach, and Ménard jumped to the beach of Dieppe.

Following a "sapper" unit moving up against the barbed wire barricade, he scouted the obstacles up beyond the beach and identified a concrete pill-box gun emplacement directly ahead about one hundred yards. Its gunners were raking the water line as the boat ramps dropped at either side.

Covering little more than a few paces, he was struck by gunfire in his right shoulder. He fell to the gravel and was conscious of no sense of pain. A man of his unit kneeled beside him, but he told him to go on. He raised himself to his feet, standing where he was, aware that the enemy fire continued to land close by, seeing chips of gravel ricochet, thinking of his medical kit, but still concentrating on the pill box ahead. He began to move forward.

A second burst of gunfire whispered past, and then Ménard was struck again, this time at the side of his face.

Crouching low, he continued moving up along the beach. One of his officers, moving up beside him, suddenly fell, both hands clutching at his midsection. Ménard looked down, then kneeled beside him and opened his medical kit. He saw the man's eyes watching his hands as he placed a morphine tablet between the fallen man's lips. The men looked at one another. Ménard nodded stiffly then rose and continued moving.

The wire had been breached, but there were wounded men along the gravel. The Lieutenant Colonel kept his eyes on the emplacement above the beach and moved forward, thinking of the fallen men and of the Major to whom he had fed the morphine tablet, who was a close friend.

He reached the parapet wall as grenades exploded within the German gun emplacement, and, not knowing how he got there, he was soon commanding operations from the cover of the broken shell of the emplacement. Using his signalman, he tried to maintain contact among the landing forces. The Fusiliers had been landed all along the beach, instead of being concentrated back of the Essex Scottish as planned. The force was broken into smaller units who moved in and joined the defenses of the Essex Scottish and the Hamiltons.

Ménard decided to move his command post

because of its limited observation, and was hit twice during the move. He fell unconscious and was taken to cover.

The major force of Les Fusiliers became divided through the different units fighting along the beach. Working through the cover of the Casino, another unit of Les Fusiliers managed to get into the town, only to be taken prisoner after a very short skirmish. The men were then able to overpower their captors, and one of them, Sergeant Dubuc, fought his way back to the beach. Another unit, led by Captain Guy Vandelac, crossed the Promenade and fell into heavy enemy gunfire before breaking out. Captain Vandelac was later reported drowned during the force withdrawal, but had actually been taken prisoner.

The tanks that had reached the Promenade began to operate along its span as self-propelled guns. Many wireless exchanges were monitored of the contacts between tank crew commanders and officers along the beach defense points, requesting cover fire or pinpointing targets. The German 37-millimeter anti-tank guns were ineffective against the armor of the Churchills, and it was not until they brought in an anti-tank unit manning 75-millimeter guns that the tanks along the Promenade began to suffer damage. The roadblock obstacles, which had prevented the Churchills from getting off the Promenade into the town, now served as a form of protection. The close range 75-millimeter guns were unable to bring their flat trajectory fire onto the

Churchills, and, aside from the few which were immobilized along the Promenade, most of the tanks withdrew to the beach.

Captain D. F. Macrae, of the Essex Scottish, pinned down with his men under the sea wall, had been greatly heartened at the moment of the landing of Les Fusiliers Mont Royal. Despite the heavy wall of gunfire, the troops had struck the beach without pause and moved up quickly despite the casualties they suffered from the instant of the landing. The initial Essex Scottish assault had quickly lost its ability to continue organized operations, and he felt the reserves might help turn the tide. But the situation rapidly became a more protracted defense than before, despite the small successful actions. Instead of two batallions pinned to the beach, there were now three.

The operational battalions were parts of two Brigades whose command groups had come ashore among the tank landing craft. Brigadier Sherwood Lett, commander of the 4th Brigade, whose command group had been on board the craft from which Lieutenant Colonel Andrew's tank had had its tragic landing accident, was unable to land. The craft that carried him, L.C.T.8, failed in its second attempt to touch down, and during this attempt Brigadier Lett was badly wounded. Through signals, he transfered command of the brigade to Lieutenant Colonel R. R. Labatt, commander of the Hamiltons on "White" Beach. The signal was received and acknowledged, but with the Hamiltons pinned down tightly by enemy fire, Labatt could hardly maintain effective supervision of operations. The command was retained by Lett, who was kept apprised of the situation. He directed what operations and movements possible from his L.C.T. close offshore as he received emergency medical attention while still under the heavy German fire that continued to fall among the support craft close to shore.

The 6th Brigade commander, Brigadier W.W. Southam, did get to the beach. In fact, he was the only officer of his command group to do so. Wounded during action on the beach, he made contact with Major G. M. Rolfe, the senior signals officer, and maintained what communications were possible, through the wireless equipment in the signals officer's scout car, with the Force Headquarters on board H.M.S. Calpe.

Brigadier Southam, with Major Rolfe in the scout car, was positioned along the beach in line with the burning tobacco factory, and had small visual command of the conditions along the west part of the beach. Along the sea wall below the Casino, the Hamiltons, with their reinforcement of the Fusiliers Mont Royal, were well entrenched in the positions of cover. But the action along the Promenade near the Casino was little more than an attempt to locate sources of enemy gunfire and call for support fire from the tanks. The condition of the wounded and the limited medical facilities on the beach made it imperative that a force be organized for their evacuation. Many of the small landing craft and support vessels were operating very close to shore, picking up what wounded men they could or providing support fire from their armament.

On board the Force Headquarters ship, reports of tanks operating along the Promenade, and of assault groups moving into the streets of Dieppe through the Casino, spurred belief among the commanders that the situation was stabilizing, and penetration to the harbor still a feasible objective.

After the committment of Les Fusiliers Mont Royal, General Roberts still had an available reserve afloat, the Royal Marine "A" Commando. At a point some time after 0800, the Royal Marine Commando were ordered into armored landing craft to go into the beach in support of the Essex Scottish. The plan was to break into the town of Dieppe and move east, through the inner streets, passing below the harbor installations, then attack the fortifications along the east cliffs in a flank assault. Consideration was given to landing the remainder of the tanks, and orders were issued. But these were rescinded ten minutes later and no further armor of the 14th Army Tank Regiment (Calgary) was sent into the beaches.

At about 0830 hours, the final assault forces of the operation approached the shoreline under cover of a heavy smoke screen put down by the Douglas Boston medium bombers. The gunfire turned on the approaching craft was as heavy as that focused on the earlier force of the Fusiliers. The German gunners had registered the range off shore by this time, and despite covering fire from the beaches, the tanks on shore, and even the support fire from the naval craft, the Marino Commando craft were under the heaviest enemy barrage that had been put down on the assault forces through the landings.

The Marine commander, Lieutenant Colonel J. P. Phillipps, approaching the barrage of destructive fire, realized the landings were futile. He made a rapid reconnaisance of the conditions along the beach from his vantage point close offshore, recognizing the static and deteriorating state of the assault. He ordered his craft slowed and stood up. Signaling broadly with his arms, he directed the craft carrying his force to come about and withdraw to the cover of the offshore smoke screen. There were seven landing craft carrying the Marine Commandos, and the officer directed that his craft make a sweep across the flotilla so his retrograde order could be seen. The German gunfire intensified with every meter the craft drew closer to the shore. Despite the increased support fire from the flak craft and the support vessels standing in alongside, the German barrage did not slacken.

Of the seven craft carrying the Marines, only three actually touched down. Under Lieutenant Colonel Phillipps' command, the rest turned away. The commander's action prevented many men of his unit from landing along a beach on which their numbers could have added little save the likelihood of compounding the number of wounded and killed.

As his own craft turned away from shore,

Lieutenant Colonel Phillipps was struck by German gunfire and mortally wounded. Among the heaviest casualties suffered along the Dieppe Beach were those incurred by the three craft that touched down carrying the Royal Marines.

By 0900 hours the reports had begun to filter through to Force Command Headquarters. Aside from the Varengeville landing by Lord Lovat's Number 4 Commandos, the other assaults had achieved, at best, very limited success in pursuing the planned objectives. The alarming news of the Royal Regiment of Canada and the Black Watch on the beach at Puys had, at this point, only been suggested by the sketchy signals that had come in. The "no sign of life on shore" signal would not reach the Calpe for close to two hours. But, beyond the faint hope of a penetration of significance, as indicated in the reports from Pourville, together with the clearly obvious situation along the main beaches, a conference among the commanders brought the suggestion from Captain Hughes-Hallet that "the withdrawal should take place with as little further delay as possible, and should be confined to personnel."

1030 hours was regarded as the earliest possible time to fix the commencement of withdrawing forces. The communications systems to "Alfred," the code name for the headquarters at Uxbridge, required substantial time for the signals to be transmitted and then the air cover groups redirected and advised. The organization and orders for the small craft that would go into the beaches had to be passed. The offshore destroyer group would lead up the naval support, standing-in as close in shore as was possible. The myriad details of this sudden and improvised containment of action and withdrawal of forces from the beaches was, if it were to succeed, almost as complex as the details that had been involved in the launching of the operation.

As the preliminary preparations for organizing the withdrawal were put into action, a signal arrived from Uxbridge that four squadrons of B-17 Flying Fortresses of the U.S. Army Air Corps, with escort squadrons of R.A.F. Spitfires, had successfully attacked the Luftwaffe installations at the aerodrome at Abbeville. The attack was reported to have been very accurate. To many of the officers and men the news became of increased significance within a very short time. The heavy air attack by the Luftwaffe had not yet begun over Dieppe, and the bombing of the Abbeville aerodrome deprived the Germans of the use of its closest major base to Dieppe for at least two hours during the critical stages of the withdrawal from the beaches.

In a final Command conference, the time for commencing the withdrawal was changed to accomodate the concern over the ability to contact the Camerons, who were at that time fighting at the crossroad of Petit Appeville, in from the beaches at Pourville. The withdrawal time was finalized for 1100 hours.

Before the withdrawal became operational, the German bombers struck in force.

14

It was past 1100 hours and Lance Sergeant Hickson and his force were still in command of the small building facing the Boulevard de Verdun. The Sergeant was seated on the floor of a room in the first storey of the building, looking across at the body of a German sniper who had been killed during the clearing operation more than an hour before. From back along the beach, the sounds of gunfire had not slackened, and now, over the sounds of guns, the men could hear the screaming drone of aircraft engines. They sounded just above the buildings.

Moving carefully to the shattered window, several of the men raised themselves to the openings, trying to see beyond the Promenade. An aircraft tore over just then, its engine seeming to hammer the sky apart, and the sound was followed briefly by a heavy explosion. The men had taken cover as the plane passed. Now they chanced another movement to the window opening. The area about the beach was completely obscured by smoke. To the right, the building with the high chimneys was burning even more fiercely than it had been an hour before. One of the men, transfixed by the scene of destruction he was watching, turned to call the Lance Sergeant's attention. Before he completed the gesture, he was thrown back from the window. The others were looking down at his suddenly still form, when another salvo of automatic weapon fire smashed against the window frame and into the room. Hickson was up and shouting to the men.

They rushed into the building corridor just before a sharp blast shook the room behind them. Outside, another bomb detonated close by, and the air shook with the sounds of aircraft engines. Bombs fell immediately after, farther away, sounding as if they had struck the beach.

Lance Sergeant Hickson led the men back toward the building entrance. From the firing just moments before, they knew there would be Germans below.

Germans were entering the building as Hickson and his men rushed down toward the entrance. The Lance Sergeant fired his Sten gun as he rushed forward, stunning the Germans in the instant. The Canadians paused briefly, firing steadily at the enemy unit, then dashed out under the building entrance and to the left. They moved slowly, under the continued firing, working their way along the Boulevard to a point across from the Casino entrance beyond the Promenade. It took them almost an hour to reach it.

From their positions of cover, the men were able to see across the Promenade and over the beach to the shoreline. The water was erupting in geysers as bombs landed among the smashed and abandoned landing craft. Small objects, looking like bits of debris, floated near the water's edge. Some were thrown aloft in the spill of the bomb explosions. A layer of smoke hung over the beach, obscuring the sun and the sky, and the low flying aircraft that they could nonetheless hear almost directly overhead. Beneath the smoke, they looked out over the water seeing movement of the flak craft and one motor gunboat speeding along the shore, its guns firing toward the east headland in the direction of the castle.

One of the men tried to say something, but could not make himself heard. The small unit huddled under cover, watching for the opportunity to dash across the Boulevard to the cover of the Casino. They saw small craft moving in toward the shore, and it occurred to several of them that the forces were beginning a withdrawal from the beaches.

On board the Calpe, landing craft had begun to come out from the beaches and move alongside to transfer wounded men onto her decks. The destroyer had moved in closer to shore, along with other support vessels. Crewmen of the destroyer helped bring the wounded on board, carrying those that could not walk to the belowdeck cover of the wardrooms. The open spaces throughout the ship began to fill with men.

Not waiting for the landing craft, some of the forces had made their way down to the water, wading out from the shoreline, signaling to passing craft, and struggling to be picked up. The smoke began to be blown inland and the sky became briefly visible over the beach. The men huddled under the sea wall looked up and could see the sky crowded with the battle of R.A.F. fighters and Germans bombers in close, small formations, moving up from the south. The fighters shaped long graceful arcs as they dove over the German craft, others coming from different places in the sky and cutting strangely frightening patterns in their maneuvers. A German Dornier came in low over the beach from behind the town and roared out over the water, disappearing into the low smoke with two British fighters trailing it. The sounds overcame the roaring gunfire for a brief time.

The medical teams continued to tend the wounded, the Hamilton's Regimental Chaplain still moving from station to station. Knowing that the evacuation was now under way, he helped the organization of the wounded down to the shoreline to the approaching craft.

The tanks that had ranged over the Promenade had moved back down to the beach area. Others had been immobilized and were abandoned above the sea wall. Their crews joined the crews of the Churchills on the beach now, moving to points where they could establish support fire for the troops during the withdrawal.

A flight of R.A.F. medium bombers flew in low, close to shore, and lay another smoke screen, but a sudden movement of wind dispersed the smoke rapidly. Through the thinning haze of the smoke, a line of landing craft began to approach the shore. Men, seeing the craft, began to run down the beach, leaving the cover of the sea wall. They were stopped briefly by a sudden frightening sound from above.

German dive bombers had broken through the

fighter cover and were streaking downward, their engines bringing a new whining shriek to the din along the beach. The JU87s came into view, shaping long steep maneuvers as they pulled out of their dives, then banking and streaking away out over the water. Bombs hit the beach and tore the shoreline apart. Streaks of orange flame shot out and were followed by slowly mushrooming clouds of smoke. The smoke cleared, leaving areas of stillness in the chaos. Broken landing craft began to litter the shore, and others, touching down and picking up men, moved out and hovered, waiting for chances to close with the waterline again and help more of the troops aboard.

A sleek motor gunboat came close to the shore, its engines let to idle out of gear, rocking heavily with the movement along its decks of crewmen and evacuees reaching down to help others aboard. Chaplain Foote carried one man out into the shallows and signaled to a naval rating to help him. The sailor lifted the wounded man from the chaplain's shoulder and set him carefully on the deck of the gunboat, then reached out to help the chaplain to board, but Chaplain Foote had moved back up on the beach, returning to the aid station to bring another man down.

A small landing craft edged into the beach close to the gunboat. There were a number of men already aboard the craft, and they called to others running along the beach. A group of soldiers ran toward the craft, wading out into the water, and began to board. The center of the craft suddenly exploded and immediately settled against the bottom. The survivors threw themselves from the craft's sides and moved off in search of other boats to carry them from the beach.

Lieutenant Colonel Ménard returned to consciousness. He was lying on his back, and very close to him the pounding of a machine gun caused a severe pain in his head. The sun was shining on him and blinding his vision, and he felt searing pain through every part of his body. He slowly opened his eyes and was looking at a helmeted naval gunner firing a mounted Bren gun. He knew then he was on a boat of some kind. The spent shells from the Bren gun's breech spilled across the deck, making small ringing sounds against metal.

A drumming series of explosions shook the boat as he lay there and then a black shadow covered the sky for an instant. He recognized the shape of a German fighter pass overhead. Higher up he could now see other aircraft, and he turned slightly, noting clearly that he was sprawled across a stack of ammunition containers. He twisted his body, trying to rise and look out over the boat's side. There was a huge cloud of smoke in the air to his left. But he could not manage to see the beach. The gunner close to him began to fire again and, after a few moments, Ménard lay back and watched the sky.

He could see German and British fighters circling high overhead. To him, it seemed that he was not part of any of this, but as if he was watching the air battle above him as a disinterested observer. He watched two small aircraft, very high up, streaking in a straight line, one directly behind the other. Then a thin trail of smoke began to stream back from the leading aircraft and, seconds later there was a silent burst of flame and the lead craft disappeared. The trailing aircraft veered away and dove toward a lower altitude. The Colonel felt an instant's panic, certain the fighter was going to crash into his boat. He could follow its complete maneuver from where he lay and saw it growing larger with frightening speed. It then changed course and banked out over him, and he recognized the insignia of the R.A.F. and the delicate silhouette of a Spitfire's wings and tail. The plane vanished from his line of sight.

The gunner stopped firing and looked down. He saw the Colonel's eyes were open and moved toward him. Without speaking he held a metal cup to Ménard's lips and cushioned the back of his head. Ménard tasted the burning sweetness of the rum, then closed his eyes in acknowledgement. The gunner nodded and smiled, offering the lip of the metal cup again Ménard signaled no, then closed his eyes again. When he looked up, the gunner was gone, but the sky was once more filled with aircraft.

Lance Sergeant Hickson had gotten across the Boulevard to the open doorways of the Casino building. It was almost deserted now, with some riflemen of the Hamiltons standing near open window frames along the east side, firing out across the Promenade. The sergeant and his group moved quickly down to the beach end of the Casino, passing the broken doorways that he had demolished with explosive charges hours ago. The gunners had dashed into the far rooms after his explosives had gone off, tossing grenades and firing their automatic weapons, clearing the snipers in the opening minutes of the assault. It seemed now as if all that had happened days ago. Now he paused briefly, then moved out with the men to the posts along the parapet, where men of the Hamiltons were beginning to make their way to the shoreline and the incoming craft that would take them off.

Captain Macrae of the Essex Scottish was at the water line of "Red" Beach. It appeared that none of the landing craft had made it to shore along this stretch of the beach and many men were running out into the water, moving along parallel to the shore, looking for the rescue craft. A German fighter made a pass across the beach and the men threw themselves to the gravel. Patterns of machine gun fire broke across the beach, and an artillery shell exploded just at the water line. A line of mortar salvos broke the surface of the water near shore, and when the surface and smoke settled Macrae thought he saw the wreckage of several landing craft floating in the suddenly calm water.

Enemy aircraft roared over the beach again and Macrae began to run eastward along the shore, hoping to locate incoming craft and direct them to where the men of the Essex Scottish were massing along the beach front. To his right, as he ran, he saw a string of shells explode among the buildings fronting the beach. He was certain they were shells of naval support guns.

Near the east end of the beach, Captain Macrae found a small rowboat upended on the gravel. Others ran up and the boat was righted, then pushed down and into the water. A shell struck the beach almost alongside. Most of the men were wounded in the explosion and Macrae helped them into the boat. He then pushed the boat out into deeper water and, clinging to its stern, began kicking and stroking with a free arm, propelling the small wooden craft away from shore. He remained in the water, pushing the boat and swimming through areas which lay clouded by dense smoke. He heard the voices of men in craft close by at times, and called out, but found no one. Finally, after maneuvering the rowboat for about two miles, they were spotted by a naval launch and picked up. Captain Macrae was the sole officer of the Essex Scottish who had landed on the beaches, that returned to England after the raid.

Farther out on the water, among the larger naval vessels, the German bombers had begun to have their effect.

15

Beneath the fighter cover provided by the Royal Air Force, the numerous operations of the early hours of 19 August, 1942, were largely unimpeded by aerial attack. By 1030 hours, however, the Germans had begun to strike with organized bomber formations, escorted by many fighters. And as the morning progressed, most of the Luftwaffe units of the western front were called into action. Bomber groups and fighter squadrons from points as distant as Belgium and the Netherlands saw action over the channel that day.

The main forces of German aerial operations arrived over the waters of the Dieppe area in the hours that the withdrawal along the main beaches began. Dive bombers attacked the approaching landing craft, followed by fighters firing cannon and machine guns. The R.A.F. cover was increased, and above the low level attacks among the surface ships and the beaches, hundreds of individual battles were fought between the escort Focke-Wulf 190s and the Spitfires. Dornier 217 bombers attacked in formations of three, breaking through the fighter cover and making their bomb runs with Spitfires trailing them down, veering off and winging over to resume their attacks. The fighting in the air was conducted mainly at low altitudes because the scattered naval forces off Dieppe, and the beaches themselves, were so obscured in the smoke of gunfire and the constantly lain smoke screens by the medium bombers and the destroyers.

From the gun positions on the destroyers, naval crews watched Dornier formations move in over the waters close to shore, fighters attacking all through the bomb runs. They saw the Dorniers come away over the water, some trailing persistent fighters who continued to maneuver over and under the bombers, firing carefully timed bursts of machine gun and cannons, then winging up and returning over the beaches to maintain their spread of cover over the withdrawing troops.

Standing on the deck of the Calpe, several officers watched a flight of six Spitfires break into formations of three and attack a formation of the Dorniers. The bombers were entering a run over Dieppe, over what appeared from the distance to be the long east-west stretch of "Red" and "White" Beaches. The bombers came in from the east, from behind the pall of smoke that hung over the coast at Puys. One of the Spitfire formations dove at the bombers from over the water, the other coming down from above and behind the formation. One of the bombers moved out from the formation, flying out over the water, two of the British fighters closing on it. A pencil thin line of smoke began to trail back from the port engine of the Dornier. It was heading west, coming directly over the naval craft off shore. As the Dornier passed over the Calpe, the fighters were firing. The gunners on the Calpe's decks followed the bomber in their gunsights, but did not fire because of the fighters. One Spitfire banked outward and up, maneuvering to resume its attack from above. At that point, the Dornier seemed to stop flying. It just came apart in the air in a burst of yellow flashes. The explosion reached the ears of the men on the Calpe instants later and they saw one wing of the bomber trailing down, flipping in a lazy pattern until it fell from sight. The two fighters roared over the destroyer as they returned to the attack.

Looking back, the men saw the fighters had disrupted the formation. The bombers had not yet reached the point over the beaches, but had broken formation, obviously taking evasive action. The attacking fighters followed them, two more out over the water, and a third turning left and disappearing behind the smoke that hung over the town.

The gunners on the destroyer now trailed the bombers and the Oerlikons began firing, tracers moving up and arcing before the path of the two German craft. The two bombers roared over the ship, their bombs having been jettisoned seconds earlier and falling into the water some hundreds of yards away. The ship rolled slightly from the impact of the exploding bombs, and then the air suddenly was clear. The aerial fight had moved to another part of the sky.

As the time of the start of the withdrawal operation came and passed, the naval craft had begun to move closer inshore. The water was beginning to mass tightly with numbers of craft working off the shore. Below the destroyer's deck, escort craft moved alongside and hove-to as men were passed from one vessel to the next. The smaller boats then eased away and steered courses back to the beaches. Fighters attacked the decks during one such transfer of wounded and evacuees. Beneath the sounds of firing from all directions now, the fighters came without warning, three abreast streaking down over the paired ships. The movement of the men crossing from one deck to another stopped in the brief moments of gunfire, the planes roaring past, portions of deck and rail splintering under the machine gunning. Two men in battledress fell to the water in the narrow space between the ships' hulls. The destroyer's pom-poms and Oerlikons were firing now, and the point where the ships were joined was suddenly clear, figures sprawled across the deck nearby, others huddled in what cover they could find against the superstructure. The space between the destroyer and the smaller craft widened suddenly as the smaller gunboat swung out in a broad turn to port, the waters along her starboard side flattening. She steered clear of several smaller craft, slowing rapidly, then came about and returned to the side of the Calpe. The transfer of men resumed, and naval crewmen carried the wounded and dead belowdeck.

The larger armed landing craft, loaded with men from the beaches, struck out into the deeper waters of the channel, making to cross to the English ports. Fighters circled overhead, but the German planes continued the attacks, fighters diving down to engage the Spitfires and bombers passing over in following formations, diving at the open craft, machine gunning from almost sea-level heights. The casualties continued to mount, even away from the beaches.

Throughout the hours of the withdrawal, the naval forces offshore remained under almost constant air attack. The men who had been transfered on the larger craft from shore began to fill the open deck space of the destroyers and launches. Fully laden landing craft hovered close beside the larger ships, waiting to offload the wounded they carried. The ships had moved still closer to the shore by now, and with the destroyer Berkeley working close to Calpe, another formation of bombers broke through the upper fighter defense screen.

The Berkeley was transfering wounded aboard from both port and starboard decks when three Dorniers roared across in close formation. Huge geysers erupted from the surface of the water as the near misses struck. And then Berkeley shuddered as a bomb struck her directly amidship. Her deck guns continued firing for a short while, then broke off as the burning began to spread the length of the ship. Landing craft and gunboats which, moments before had been transfering men onto Berkeley's deck, now moved in close against the destroyer's sides and began taking soldiers and naval men off. The destroyer Calpe herself came close alongside, circling the Berkeley slowly, the deck guns firing steadily into the sky overhead. Men were being pulled from the water alongside the Berkeley's hull. The destroyer, struck only moments before, had already begun to settle. Her decks were almost awash, and men leaving the sinking craft merely stepped across to the low decks of the support vessels alongside or into the water. Naval personnel worked hurriedly, transfering the wounded to landing craft, clearing the last living survivors from Berkeley's decks. Through the whole operation, Calpe continued to circle slowly, her guns now keeping the skies overhead clear.

When the decks of the Berkeley were at last emptied, the escort and support craft stood off to some distance and Calpe moved in, positioning herself broadside at close range. Her forward and midship guns swung slowly, the barrels lowering to maximum depression, almost deck level. A strangely inexplicable moment of silence hung over this maneuver. Then, on command, the Calpe's guns began firing. The Berkeley was shrouded in a cover of dense smoke as the 4-inch guns continued firing shells into the hull of the mortally damaged destroyer. The firing broke off and Calpe stood away. When the gunfire smoke had cleared, the Berkeley was settling rapidly, her midsection already below the water, the fires along her superstructure still billowing heavy black smoke. Within sight of the Berkeley, time seemed to suddenly become suspended as the men along the decks of ships standing off watched the destroyer slowly settle beneath the surface. Finally, geysers of trapped air and debris rising to the surface and a spreading cover of black oil, marked the spot where she had been. The men became aware that the gunfire had not stopped, the aircraft had not ended their attacks, the Spitfires maintaining the high cover were still circling far above. And down low over the level of the ship's decks, Focke-Wulf 190s were crossing over, coming from out over the channel, Spitfires diving on them from above. The German fighters tore over the cluster of ships, machine guns roaring, the craft banking up into the gunfire of the Spitfires. Then a second flight bore in rapidly, their gunfire raking the Calpe's deck and superstructure. Small explosions above told that the bridge had been hit. The fighters vanished in over the beaches, and men, rushing up the ladderways to the bridge deck, found that Air Commodore Cole had been severely wounded. He was carried belowdeck, and Calpe swung her bow in toward the beaches.

Moving to within visual range of the beach, the destroyers watched the continued Hurricane fighter sorties against the German strongpoints. The fighter attacks on the beaches in support of the raiders, which had begun moments after dawn, had continued unabated through the entire operation. They provided perhaps the most effective support to the forces on the beach. The Fighter Controllers in both Calpe and the auxiliary command craft Fernie, under Brigadier Mann, had transmitted hundreds of requests from beach positions, directing the Hurricanes and the Douglas Bostons into attacks and smoke-laying sorties. Their running reports and signal calls on incoming enemy aircraft had dispatched fighters to interceptor attacks during the hours of enemy air activity, and a very effective signals net had been maintained with their fighter control counterparts at the force headquarters at Uxbridge.

The controllers had, in fact, maintained a constant flow of information about the increased enemy air activity in the last hours, and Fighter Command at Uxbridge had committed greater numbers of fighters to air cover operations. The time lags necessitated by the transmission and retransmission of signals, and the following delays while the newly committed aircraft were alerted and made airborne, plus the time elapsed during their cross channel flight and arrival, had all accounted for the heavy numbers of German craft that had attacked the ships and beaches with relative freedom in the beginning of the attack. Now the skies were returning to the relative normalcy that had prevailed through the earlier hours of the raid.

But Dorniers and Focke-Wulfs continued to get through the defenses, though in fewer numbers as the time passed.

The withdrawals from the beach continued in masses of confusion and gunfire, and men continued to die.

16

On the beach at Dieppe, the Churchill tanks had withdrawn from the Promenade. They were ranged across the length of "Red" and "White" Beaches now, their guns turned toward the buildings beyond the promenade and the other emplacements to the east. Twenty seven tanks had been put ashore from the L.C.T.s, the better number of them having fought their way up from the beach and onto the Promenade. The concrete roadblocks erected by the Germans had effectively prevented their further penetration of the town of Dieppe, but ranging as self propelled weapons they provided excellent close-in support to the forces that occupied the Casino, and the small units that did manage to get beyond the Boulevard de Verdun.

Now, in the hours of the withdrawal, the men of the Calgary Tank Regiment formed the foundation of the beach defenses, coordinating their firepower as the larger German weapons were moved up against the men in the beach positions under the sea wall. Along the beach they continued to maneuver as fire missions were requested. One by one, the Churchills were damaged or immobilized by gunfire shattering their treads. Some became stalled in the loose gravel of the beach and were unable to move.

But even in their immobile positions, they continued to operate as gun positions.

Men at radio monitors heard the numerous exchanges between the tank crews, which continued until 1225 hours, after the withdrawal had ended. The tank men of the 14th Calgary Regiment actually provided the rear guard action along the beaches of Dieppe, remaining with their craft until all action on the beaches had ceased. Almost none of the men of the Calgary unit returned to England.

Under the cover fire from the tanks, men of the Royal Hamilton Light Infantry worked their way from the cover of the sea wall and down to the beachfront. The assault craft that had been sent in to bring the men out were standing close in under very heavy German gunfire. Rushing air attacks by the Focke-Wulfs had had a great effect of disorganizing and scattering among the craft. Some of the boats moved in toward assigned beaches, while others, driven by air attacks and the general conditions of battle, which had by this time extended well out over the water, found themselves approaching the shore along beaches to which they had not been assigned. Many craft were destroyed and never reached the evacuation beaches.

Of the eight craft dispatched from H.M.S. Prince Charles to evacuate the Essex Scottish from "Red" Beach, six were destroyed before approaching the beach. The craft from H.M.S. Prince Leopold had been ordered to "Red" Beach as well, but in the passage lost their way and beached their craft at Pourville, on "Green" Beach. In their repeated returns to the beaches, one of these assault boats is recorded as having put in at "Red" Beach late in the evacuation.

It was now close to 1200 hours and on board the command destroyer, word had finally been signalled to Calpe by Lieutenant Commander H. W. Goulding, the Senior Officer Blue Beach Landings, of the futile pass across the beach at Puys. He had been on board Calpe earlier, when the first intimations of the fate of the Royal Regiment and the Black Watch of Canada had been transmitted in the fragmented signals by way of the destroyer Garth. At General Roberts orders, he had returned to Blue Beach command and supervised the attempt to withdraw the Royals and the Black Watch. In the latter stages of the "Blue" Beach operation, Lieutenant Commander Goulding personally commanded the motor launch that approached the beach, made its searching sweep across the waters close to shore, and came under heavy enemy gunfire. It was after this sweep, at approximately 1145 hours, with four assault craft from the Princess Astrid, that the message was flashed: "Fire from beach was still terrific." One of the assault boats had been lost to enemy fire. And "there was no sign of life on the beach."

The Pourville withdrawals were proceeding effectively, despite heavy enemy activity along the beaches. With signals confirming the unfortunate circumstances at Berneval, in which only the twenty man force under Major Young had been able to withdraw, and the successful withdrawal of Lord Lovat's Number 4 Commando from Varengeville (some of whose forces had been transfered by smaller craft to the decks of the Calpe), the operational concern now centered on the main beaches of Dieppe.

The German air attacks, though now gradually being neutralized by the increased numbers of R.A.F. fighters operating over the beaches, had had a tragic effectiveness in disorganizing logistical control of the landing craft operating in the withdrawal. Despite naval barrages and the close-in work of the gunboats and flak ships, the havoc spread through aerial bombardment and machine gun attacks had destroyed great numbers of craft and, across much of the Dieppe beaches, overpowered the succession of events along the shoreline. Commander H. V. P. McClintock, the Boat Pool Officer, signalled to Calpe a message advising on the aerial domination over the beaches. The message, directed to the Naval Force Commander's Chief of Staff, was acknowledged, and the reply made, at 1220 hours: "Continue further efforts at withdrawal operations."

Those men reaching the beach now found that whatever craft were laid in along the shoreline were destroyed, and because of the damage they had sustained, unseaworthy. Many moved into the waters clinging to floating bits of debris, propelling themselves away from the beaches in hope of being picked up by other craft farther offshore. Some small boats of local origin were also employed by troops in reaching the support craft.

Captain Hughes-Hallet, concerned that the order to continue withdrawal activity might only result in further losses to the troops already embarked on landing craft, amended the order to Commander McClintock: "If no further evacuation possible withdraw."

The message, relayed through smaller craft and then transmitted to Commander McClintock, arrived with the opening word omitted: "No further evacuation possible withdraw."

This signal was exchanged at approximately 1225 hours.

Even prior to its delivery, the Boat Pool Officer had arrived at the decision that there was no further point in persisting at evacuation efforts. As a consequence, after this time, no assault or landing craft were dispatched to the shore to pick up forces.

17

Along the beaches, where no word had yet been received of the cessation of withdrawal efforts, men were still moving toward the water. The improvised aid stations near the inner entrances of the Casino were still filled with wounded, and Honorary Captain Foote continued his efforts to help the men who could not move by themselves down to where whatever evacuation craft appeared could help them off the beach. He enlisted the aid of several unwounded men and a series of carrying parties began an organized removal of all the men in the aid post.

The Germans had moved forces closer toward the Promenade, using the concrete road blocks as covering. The Churchills within range of the road beyond the Promenade set down a strong pattern of cover fire, their shells penetrating between the heavy pyramid shapes. One tank crew followed the movements of a German 37-millimeter gun and its service crew as it was slowly manhandled across the Boulevard de Verdun, firing erratically as the gun showed for moments between the blocks. The tankers saw member of the German gun crew hit and fall, others rushing out from enemy points to replace them, and the gun continued to be moved forward.

Several of the Churchills were firing at once, and

with the concentration of their gunnery it seemed incredible that the gun had not yet been stopped. In a final rush, the Germans moved the gun forward again to within yards of the open space behind the roadblocks. Their determination to position the gun had obviously blinded them to how open a position they had chosen. On signals between two crew commanders in the tank, firing was broken off briefly. Between them, the position of the two tanks could converge from both sides of the roadblock back of which the gun was being positioned. They stopped and waited, permitting the gunners to manipulate the 37-millimeter anti-tank weapon into position. Machine gun fire from the buildings beyond the Boulevard covered the German movement.

Troops of the Hamiltons, dug in along the beach, watched apprehensively as the gun continued to move forward. From their positions of cover under the sea wall, they could see Germans moving freely now along the Boulevard, but did not fire. They did not want to draw the German fire from the upper floors of the buildings, or reveal their positions. These remaining forces on the beach, with their officers, acknowledged to themselves the difficulty of where they were in relation to the stretch of gravel they would have to cross to reach the water's edge. Several groups received orders to move out when the tanks began to fire again. Others remained, the indecision caused by the density of machine gun fire along the open spaces of the beach forcing them to hold to cover, to delay their movement for as long as they could.

The 37-millimeter gun stopped moving finally.

Hamiltons watched the German crews hurriedly position the gun, and ammunition bearers dashed up from across the road, bent low, their large round helmets almost totally obscuring their faces, their arms hung straight down, carrying shells and charges. Three bearers ran in a column. As the first reached the new gun position, the troops watching from the sea wall had their lines of sight suddenly obscured by a rush of explosions in and around the roadblock directly in front of the 37-millimeter gun. The men in the Churchills had resumed their firing.

The small barrage continued for perhaps thirty seconds, then stopped. As the smoke and powdered debris began to clear, no sign could be seen of the German gun, or of its service crew. A cheer went up along the sea wall, and the regularity of the Churchill gunfire began again.

A lone Dornier made a pass along the length of the beach, its lower bomb door hanging open. But no bombs fell. Men looking up saw the port engine of the German craft trailing heavy black smoke. The sound of the engines was deafening, even over the continual din of the exchange of fire on the beach. Several troops rolled over and fired their small arms up as the Dornier passed over, knowing they could have little effect, but firing out of senses of protective instinct. The bomber flew out of sight over the east end of the beach, and gunfire from the troops followed it the entire way. A huge explosion followed almost immediately after it went out of sight, but only those along the east end of the beach were aware of it. They thought the bomber may have crashed, but were not sure.

Honorary Captain Foote had dropped the man he was carrying as the plane came over. He threw himself across the figure, covering his head as he did. As soon as the roar of the aircraft began to lessen, he rose and continued his progress down to the water carrying the wounded Hamilton.

A small assault craft had edged into the beachfront, and men, seeing it, began to run toward it. Machine gunners beyond the Promenade, seeing the rush of movement, raised their range of fire and concentrated their guns along the water's edge. Men dropped among the running, but the others did not stop. Had they been conscious of it, they would have heard the sudden rise in return fire from the sea wall and from the few Churchill tanks that were still operating. But the protective gunfire did little good. Most of the troops running toward the craft were cut down along the water's edge, some falling into the water, raising themselves and moving forward only to collapse again and be drowned.

Captain Foote was near the shore where the craft had touched in. He had lowered the man he was carrying, and had himself taken cover by flattening himself against the gravel in the minute ridge directly on the waterline. Fine glistening wet pebbles pressed against the side of his face. He heard the hammering against the gravel as the machine gun rounds struck close to him, even felt the drumming of mens' boots as they ran along the shore. A figure loomed over him and fell, covering his head and pressing his face into the water. He coughed and fought to raise himself, struggling slowly, until once again able to breathe. He twisted his body and eased the fallen figure away, then rose to his knees. There were bodies all around him that had not been there ten seconds before. Finding a sense of meaninglessness in what he did, he groped for the man he had been carrying earlier, examining the faces of the men laying sprawled close to him.

He had earlier become expert in identifying the look of the dead. Now his eyes, no longer registering the horror that had buried itself somewhere very deep within him, sought among the fallen men for expressions of response, signs of the living. He thought he heard an anguished moan and looking carefully, saw movement in one man's eye. He freed him from the mass of fallen figures and moved away, dragging the wounded soldier along. The assault craft had moved slightly offshore and he heard men shouting. One man screamed loudly very close to his face, and the Chaplain called to the men in the craft. The hull of the small boat edged in closer and two men reached out to grasp Captain Foote's shoulder. He shook them loose and indicated the two wounded he was holding up. Hands reached down and dragged the figures over the side of the craft. Looking up, the Chaplain saw the men signaling for him to follow. The craft was full to the point of instability, its hull sitting so low that water lapped over the gunwale edges. The Captain shook his head, then turned away. Several more men had run down into the water. He helped them push the craft off and, seeing them grasp tightly to fixtures along the boat's edge, continued pushing until he was chest high in the water.

Some of the men were still calling to him, but he

could not make out what they were saying. Another aircraft passed over the beach at that moment, and the captain backed away. The assault craft's engine rumbled and gears were engaged. The shape of the hull receded to deeper waters, men hanging by holds along its sides, still in the water, but moving off with the overloaded craft. Captain Foote stood there until the craft faded into the pall of smoke some thirty yards offshore, then turned and walked back up to the water's edge. Among the fallen dead, many men kneeled or sat in total exhaustion. Some were still watching the edges of mist out over the water, waiting for more evacuation craft to appear. Others, seemingly no longer able to hope, merely stared blank-eyed. The concentration of machine gun fire had moved off.

Honorary Captain Foote continued his work moving the wounded to positions of cover and administering what emergency aid he could. When the last craft had landed, and it became clear that evacuation efforts had come to an end, Captain Foote refused to embark on the last craft he was able to approach with more wounded. He refused the offer of a space that was being made for him, and retreated from the waterline, where he joined the groups of wounded still under cover under the sea wall. He was among those taken prisoner, and survived the war. He was subsequently awarded the Victoria Cross.

18

Not yet aware that evacuation efforts were being stood down, Captain Hughes-Hallet ordered Calpe to come about and lay a screen of smoke to cover the final withdrawal movements. The destroyer raised steam, lay over to starboard and began to race seaward, a heavy cloud of white smoke issuing from her funnel and laying out softly across the surface of the water. On deck some of the men began to cheer. They were under the impression they were heading out into the channel and back to England.

They passed one destroyer working slowly to port and starboard, her forward 4-inch gun still moving, its muzzle pointed skyward at the circling aircraft overhead. But the planes were Spitfires. There seemed to be no Germans in the sky now.

On deck, among the mass of men huddled against the gunwales along the after deck, four men stood close to one another. Their uniforms, beneath the combat gear, were those of the United States Army. Americans from the 1st U.S. Ranger Battalion, they had gone ashore early in the raid with Number 4 Commando at Varengeville. Two sergeants and two Corporals, their names were Brady, Stemson, Szima, and Koons. They said little, even to one another, but continued to look out across the water as the destroyer made speed. Looking up, they watched the heavy trail of smoke as it fell away behind them and spread on the water. They could not see the shore, but heard the sudden rush of calling as German aircraft were spotted moving down on them.

The rhythmic thudding of the pom-pom guns began shaking the deck. The quad-mounted small caliber guns fired in pairs, first the upper guns, then the lower, in rapid sequence. The sound of these guns was curiously unlike any the Americans had heard before. The German fighters tore over the ship's decks, but had miscalculated their approach and were far wide of a line of flight that would have allowed them to rake the destroyer with machine gun fire.

The heavier bore Oerlikons began firing now, their muzzles following the Focke-Wulfs. The planes bore off and did not make a second sweep.

The Americans raised their heads, trying to see the German fighters. Remembering perhaps, earlier in the day, after scaling the cliffs at Vasterival and moving in on the German machine gun emplacement, how two Spitfires had appeared as if out of nowhere. They roared upward over the crest of the cliff, then banked and fell away, coming around again and sweeping in abreast, their gunfire converging forcefully on the area in and around the pill box.

Snipers had been firing the whole time and they were unable to see the action clearly. But remembering now, watching the British commando coolly working his way up a powerline pole, snipers firing continually, and cutting communications and power lines, then coming back down, jumping lightly clear to the ground, and smiling in a forced air of nonchalance. Or the British Sergeant Major who had been hit and whom Corporal Koons carried away from the action. The Sergeant Major shouted constantly at Koons, ordering him to drop him and fall to cover. And, as if he had mystically anticipated the action, German firing had cut across their line of withdrawal. The Sergeant Major, painfully wounded, continued indicating targets as they bore him down to the waiting craft, even shouting loudly for cover fire as the assault craft edged out from the Varengeville beach.

The aircraft sounds had made them remember the relief of being on the water again after the dawn action. And it made them remember the dead they had left behind, and how the sudden explosion on the cliff, when the gun batteries blew, had thrown off the fire of a German machine gunner and probably saved them. Now one of the sergeants wanted a cigarette badly. But nobody had any, and they were standing near ammunition cases, in any event. The thought of possibly causing an explosion by lighting a cigarette struck the sergeant strangely and he laughed.

Calpe slowed, stopped making smoke, and came about again. Returning toward the coast, she passed the destroyer they had seen earlier. Signals were flashed by Aldis lamp, repeated on the wireless, and passed to the Commanders: The Boat Pool Officer had signaled to the assault craft to stand down all movement toward the beach.

Calpe acknowledged the signal, then continued her course inshore, the signal lamps still flashing. She was ordering all large craft inshore to establish a barrage to cover the withdrawing craft. Men all over the deck were alarmed at the reversal of the ship's course. They had by then concluded the ship was steering for the outer channel and they were finished with Dieppe. But now, heading back in, unaware of the circumstances of the new course, they feared reentry into the battle. Some of the troops on board had come off the beaches at Pourville, others, like the American Rangers, had been at Varengeville and Vasterival. But most of the men along the decks had been at "White" Beach. Large numbers of them had virtually swum away from the battle in the broken assault craft, hanging by strands of line while holding themselves as far down in the water as possible to avoid enemy gunfire. They could not believe they were being returned to that inferno. The ship steamed into the clouds of the smoke screen it had just set over the water. And, listening carefully, the men along the decks began to hear the distant sounds of gunfire. Their ears, acute now to the different rhythms and reports, recognized small arms, Thompsons, and Sten guns, and the tearing chatter of the German MG 42 machine guns.

They were, they knew, once again close inshore off the beaches of Dieppe. Smaller naval craft still hovered nearby, but they could not see the beach, only listen to the thunder of the guns coming through the heavy smoke and mist.

About a thousand feet overhead, a Dornier flew

in from over the water. The men took rapid cover, but they then saw one engine of the bomber trailing smoke, and its bomb doors hung open. A Spitfire banked away from behind the German, then a second roared into a turning climb. And the sky was clear again, except for the high circling fighters.

More of the small craft that had come out from shore now moved across the water, approaching already heavily laden support craft. One L.C.T., moving deep and slow in the water, its bow pushing out a thick sluggish bow wave, moved out toward the open water being towed by a larger ship. Their movement was heavy and lumbering, the L.C.T.'s sides perilously low to the waterline. But the channel had remained miraculously calm all through the day. The guns of the Calpe began to fire toward the shore as the men along the deck watched the L.C.T. being towed out to sea.

It appeared that the last of the assault craft that had touched in at the beach were now moving out to the area of water where the destroyer sat, facing broadside to the coast, her full firepower blasting at the unseen targets inland, the emplacements near the Castle, the artillery stations along the cliff in from the west headland. Men on deck thought they could hear the reports of the shells landing, but were not sure. They watched the small craft moving across the water near them, oblivious to the roar of the Calpe's guns or those of two more destroyers that had moved up now.

A small, sleek patrol boat stirred the waters alongside Calpe. She flew the French *tricolor* at her stern. Men of the naval crew recognized her as one of the *chasseurs* of the fleet force. Their original task, as written into the battle order, had been to carry the Royal Marine "A" Commandos into Dieppe's inner harbor past the mole, and attack the shipping along the south wharves and the Gare Maritime. They had requested, and been given permission, to forego regulation helmets and wear brightly colored headgear so the Germans would know that Frenchmen were among the raiders.

With the ultimate abandonment of the harbor raid, they had served as liaison craft, and as support for the assault boats in the landings. Through the withdrawal they had made repeated approaches to the coast, leading evacuation craft in, escorting them away from the beaches, and, ultimately, carrying away survivors themselves. Now the small patrol boat moved past the Calpe and they could see, lined along her decks, many men in Canadian battle dress. Some of the men along the deck of the Calpe waved, but on the *chasseur* no one waved back. The French craft moved beyond Calpe and steered close to one of the assault craft, slowing as she came alongside. Someone on her bridge began calling out through a megaphone. Nothing could be heard of what had been shouted, but from the assault craft they saw a line cast. The action almost capsized the overloaded craft. The smaller vessel was drawn alongside and the men began to climb over the rail, others at the *chasseur*'s stern reaching over and helping to lift the wounded across. The transfer took several minutes and shellfire began to land while both craft were stationary. Columns of water erupted close to the *chasseur*. She rocked slightly on the disturbed water, but the transfer of the men did not stop. A shell struck the bow of the small patrol boat, causing her to drift to port. One man was seen to fall into the water, just before flames sprang up and smoke covered the forward section of the craft. The men were by now all clear of the assault craft and she was cut loose, let to drift free as the *chasseur* got under way. As she sailed clear of the smoke billowing from her own bow, the men on the Calpe could see the extent of the damage.

The upper section of the bow was no longer there, and fire rushed up from somewhere below deck forward. Men at the bow were working rapidly to suppress the flames, and the craft was now steaming down by her stern, the bow high out of the water. As she passed from view of the Calpe's deck, she was still afire, but making headway, steering out into the Channel.

The Calpe's guns broke off their fire a short time later, and she began to move slowly forward. The abandoned assault craft was washed outward by her bow wave, and she steamed slowly toward where two more assault craft loaded with men waited to be picked up. Under the sounds of the destroyers close by, whose guns were still firing, the engine telegraph could be faintly heard. The Calpe moved closer to the two craft, barely drifting now. The men in the craft worked themselves along the ship's hull, pulling hand over hand against Calpe's plating, until they came alongside the boarding ramp. Men on the deck rushed to the side and helped the men aboard. They were Hamiltons, and some Royal Marines. Bandages from medical kits had soaked through over the wounds of some of the men, their faces contorted with pain as they moved through the gunwale passage and onto the deck. Litters were brought forward and passed down to the assault craft and men were bound securely and raised up to waiting crewmen and soldiers who had come forward to help in the transfer.

Orders were being called down from the bridge, and as one of the ratings was about to cast the line of a craft loose, a boatswain stopped him. They began to tow the empty assault craft forward. Some of the men on deck, curious at what was being done, followed along to help. When the second assault craft was emptied of soldiers, it, too, was towed forward.

Crewmen jumped from the deck of the destroyer, landing in the assault craft and, working quickly at bow and stern of the smaller craft, began to lash the vessels alongside, astride the bow of the destroyer. Their duties completed, the sailors returned on board as Calpe got under way again slowly, her bow turning once again toward the shore.

19

From the command post set up by Brigadier Southam, the wireless contact through to the Calpe communications network remained clear and active. Operators transcribed the frequent signals as the commander of the 6th Brigade gave a running commentary of the final actions along the beach.

He spoke of the movement still observed along the western end of "White" Beach, where cover from the Casino building still provided avenues by which men were making their way to the water line.

Reports came through the Calpe's wireless of the work of men in the Engineer Company, and the calm, steady control of the tank crews, the handling of their guns despite all movement by the Churchills having stopped.

Reports that several assault craft could be seen close along the shore affirmed the decision made moments before by the Commanders on board Calpe.

The crews of the Churchills were seen, through these final minutes, to break off their firing, and after brief periods of time, emerge from their tanks and move off to higher points along the beach under the sea wall. Men were still firing small arms from the Casino, and away in the east, the force of gunfire from among the cover points of the Essex Scottish had remained heavy. Requests for cover fire to be placed over the control points of "Red" Beach, to divert enemy guns from the concentration of Essex Scottish troops, were transmitted to other destroyers offshore. With no artillery observation communications, the barrage would be of questionable value, but the fire missions were implemented, and in moments shells rushed overhead toward the enemy positions in the east headland beyond the harbor.

From the beaches, the men could still see the air cover of fighters circling. It extended the hope that more landing craft were approaching the shore. They moved east slowly, under cover of the sea wall, holding, then trying to resume movement, trying to reach the points beyond the end of the Promenade where cover from the Casino building offered greater protection. Gun positions along the sea wall had increased their fire now that the Churchills were no longer covering the German positions beyond the Boulevard. When the men rose slightly to fire, they still could not see the Germans.

The naval barrage continued overhead, but down at the waterline, only broken and abandoned assault craft were visible. Groups of men were huddled along the shoreline, but the men under the sea wall, looking there, could see little movement, if any. At the distance, they could not make up their minds if they were looking at dead men. One Churchill tank, up near the sea wall, had become immobilized by almost overturning into a deep depression in the gravel. It stood silent now, its right tread buried deeply, the vehicle almost upended, its long gun barrel pointed toward the ground. The tank shuddered suddenly as a German shell struck its side. Another shell sent gravel bursting outward and the orange flash of the nearby explosion blinded those who were watching. The shells began to fall more heavily along the beach just below the sea wall and the men huddled closely against the stonework. The Germans were responding to the renewed naval shelling by leveling artillery along the beach.

It was a silent exchange, under the guns, in which the Navy was being advised by its enemy that it could preserve life by ranging off. Or so, at least, were the thoughts of one of the Hamilton Lieutenants as he crouched under the sea wall and watched the renewed barrage. He had, moments earlier, completed a series of mental images of a night in London, just eight days earlier, when he had made love to an English girl whose face he never saw and whose name he knew now he would never know. And she had been the first woman to whom he had ever made love. He was, in his mind, thankful now, thinking of the girl and what he could remember of her, and of the brief time they had been together. At least, he thought, he would die if he had to, with the knowledge of what it was to be with a girl. His celibacy had been his long dark secret, but among his fellow officers he had maintained an air of urbanity which he knew had been regarded as questionable. But now, accept it or no, he thought, if I die, at least I will die a man. And not because of the pips on my epaulettes or the rounds of ammunition I have fired here on this damned beach.

It seemed strange to him now, with a sudden

internal awareness that he was going to die, that he should be thinking so strongly about someone he had known for little more than an hour. If I were to get out of this, he wondered, could I find her again?

He had seen to the needs of his men, who were almost completely out of ammunition. He ducked low as a shell landed closer than the rest. A man crouched alongside him slowly rolled forward and fell to the gravel. He reached forward, but could see the man was dead. He could see his face and did not recognize him. Out beyond the shelling, down past where the men lay flat against the gravel on the waterline, the lieutenant trained his eye on the shape of a tank landing craft that had sunk in the shallows just offshore.

If I was down there, he thought, I could work my way past the hull of the L.C.T. and swim out. There must be boats out there, else why would they continue shelling like this?

In his deeper thoughts, he knew it was all over, but he continued to stare at the L.C.T. and the possibilities it offered to reach the withdrawal craft. And he thought of London.

Another shell struck and a man along the line beneath the sea wall began to scream. No one did anything to stop the screaming and the lieutenant began to move closer to where the man huddled, his head low, his body heaving with the effort of his outcries. The lieutenant reached him and touched his shoulder, then gripped him tightly. The other man turned to look at him, and seeing the man's eyes the lieutenant's face softened. The eyes were staring, seeing nothing. But the gesture of gripping his shoulder had stopped the calling out. He drew the man close against the sea wall and once again huddled himself under cover.

Below the Casino, another L.C.T. was beached. It had begun to burn some time before, and smoke still rose up in a slowly furling column. The lieutenant now concentrated on the burning L.C.T. and did not think about the men along the shoreline who, he was sure, were dead. Nor was he thinking any longer of the girl in London.

The German guns had suddenly stopped firing at the beach.

In the Calpe, the communications operator heard the report from Brigadier Southam's scout car command post, logged it, and delivered a copy to the Commanders.

The Germans were beginning to close in on the men along the beach.

20

With the remainder of the naval force withdrawing from the shore and the signal received that an order had been broadcast cancelling further efforts by landing craft to approach the beaches, the Commanders on board Calpe resisted the idea of total withdrawal while any remote hope remained of bringing off what men were still on the beach. From Calpe's station close inshore, they could now see the numerous craft coming about in long, seemingly reluctant turns away from the French coast and moving out into the Channel.

The Commanders had held a final conference and struck on a last expedition into the beach. Calpe herself, with landing craft lashed along her bows, would make a final pass across the beaches.

The decks of the Calpe were already crowded with evacuees. The cabins and spaces belowdecks were filled almost to capacity with wounded. Medical staffs were working steadily, providing emergency aid. They were being assisted by unwounded officers and men, ship stewards of the Calpe's crew, even some of the newspaper correspondents who were now on board. Word was passed through the ship that the operation was ended, and that Calpe would make this final approach to the beach.

During the preceding hour, other destroyers had worked close into shore, one, the Brocklesby, had actually reported having grounded briefly during a change of course. Captain Hughes-Hallet contacted the commander of the gunboat Locust. The Locust was a shallow draft vessel that had been working inshore all through the operation. She would have the most recent information on what conditions were like on shore.

Abovedecks, lying under cover of passageway openings and other superstructure, men who had been transfered on board from smaller vessels hardly stirred as the Calpe swung her bow inshore. The faces of the men were blank, smeared with grime or the residue of the camouflage coloring they had applied the night before. They were the faces of the dead, expressionless and shocked in the aftereffect of the memories that were harbored beneath the surfaces of their minds. Their bodies stirred, not in response to their inner commands, but to the automatic reflexes that had become almost instinctive through the hours since dawn. A sound of gunfire, and the figures drew into themselves. Their actions in taking to maximum cover was barely in conscious response to the resumption of diving aircraft that were now approaching Calpe from over the cliffs to the east headland. Their bodies had been ordered to cover so many times at the sound of roaring engines that the reaction was automatic.

Four Focke-Wulfs made diving passes, their guns hammering as they flew across the destroyer. Some of the men looked up, their eyes blinking now in reaction to the vibrations through the ship of the incessant pom-pom guns and Oerlikons. The forward 4-inch gun battery was firing as the fighters returned for another pass. High above them, the R.A.F. fighters still circled, and they saw a formation of them wing over and dive toward the beach, then swing wide in a circling maneuver. They came out of the low turn and their formation had changed. Now the Spitfires were flying level and four abreast, streaking out from over the land toward Calpe. They roared in as the Focke-Wulfs completed the second pass over the ship, and suddenly eight fighters were involved in complicated turns and climbing maneuvers. Because of their low altitude, the aircraft soon vanished from the line of sight of those on deck. But the vibrations of the gunfire did not diminish.

Calpe moved slowly toward the shore, her bow pointed toward the east end of "Red" Beach and the harbor breakwater. Shells from the shore installations threw high columns of water as they struck, and now, closing with the shore, the machine gunners began to fire.

Men were seen clinging to an overturned raft and the ship eased carefully about, maneuvering herself between the men in the water and the shore. The men were lifted from the water, and the ship coasted slowly ahead, once more directing her bow toward the harbor breakwater. The men across the decks were now moving to the port quarter of the ship, the side facing away from the gunfire.

The forward 4-inch battery began to fire rapid salvos and shells erupted along the stone breakwater. Machine gunners emplaced along the breakwater returned the fire as the ship approached. By moving behind armor plating screens and into hatchways behind bulkheads, those on deck found cover. The machine gun fire sounded dully as it struck along the metalwork of the ship, and splinters of deck were torn and thrown upward. The destroyer stood off the breakwater briefly and continued firing. Along the starboard quarter, the ship's guns were shelling the installations above the beach. Then, slowly, Calpe executed a turn to starboard and began a pass along the beach. Her speed suddenly rose.

In the communications room the wireless operators had just passed a message to the Commanders. It was 1310 hours, and the message was from Brigadier W. W. Southam, still in the scout car with Major Rolfe on the beach below the burning tobacco factory. The message stated, simply: "Our people here have surrendered."

Calpe moved along the beach, hardly visible for the layers of smoke hanging over the surface of the water. She made for deeper waters, still steaming along the coast, passing "White" Beach without seeing the shore. Then, slowing to cast the lashed craft along the bows adrift, she turned and bore out on a course away from the coast. Behind her, columns of smoke still rose from Dieppe, and far overhead, the circling Spitfires had once more gained control of the air. There seemed to be no German aircraft in the area now.

Gunfire could still be heard from along the coast, but the German artillery was wide of its mark. No tell-tale geysers of water erupted around the destroyer. The waters about where Calpe steamed was free of moving naval craft. They moved out, and, as if reluctant to leave in the knowledge of so many men still back there on the beaches, cut a course change to the east, slowing as she cruised, in the hope of finding yet other craft that carried men from the beaches.

The gunfire from shore trailed off gradually to total silence. Smoke still hung heavily across the water and Calpe, some distance from the coast now, tracked slowly through the water, passing abandoned craft, seeing bits of debris floating, and moved slowly past a capsized assault craft from which hung the lifeless form of a man in battledress. He had used a length of line to bind his wrist to a metal ring along the overturned craft's side. But the line hung slack, its other end bound to the wrists of the figure, floating still and face-down in the water.

Observers had marked the time of the last sound of German gunfire. It was 1358 hours.

The men along the deck looked back at the capsized craft with the lifeless figure floating beside it as Calpe, at 1400 hours, stood away from the French coast.

General Roberts had framed a message to Headquarters 1st Canadian Corps. It was dispatched from the destroyer across the Channel by pigeon.

Very heavy casualties in men and ships. Did everything possible to get men off but in order to get any home had to come to sad decision to abandon remainder. This was joint decision by Force Commanders. Obviously operation completely lacked surprise.

21

Across the Channel, at Newhaven and Portsmouth, the receiving stations were being readied. The silence along the docksides among the transport and surplus personnel of the units who had been left behind almost bespoke the ominous notes in the early reports that had filtered through from command headquarters at Uxbridge.

After 1100 hours, medical staffs and orderlies, alerted at Newhaven, could be seen standing outside the casualty station, a large hall close to the docks. They spoke quietly but frequently, their eyes turned east to the horizon across the water. Waiting officers also watched the Channel, standing in quiet groups, smoking, rarely speaking. The movement of vehicles provided almost the only sound to intrude on the stillness that had settled over the waterfront of the small port.

The air activity over the Channel had been heavy all morning. Flights of fighters could be seen traveling east at high altitudes with almost predictable regularity at thirty minute intervals. And occasional formations flew in from over the water, coming low from the south. Careful observers could note, if the fighters flew closely enough over the coast as they approached, that some of the planes bore traces of battle, torn metal surfaces, punctured wings and tail sections. The engines of some of the aircraft sounded unsteady, the formations were fragmented, and the coastal watchers were reminded of the returning fighters after the massive air battles over the Channel through the summer of 1940.

Ambulances in convoy began to line the motor parks along the docksides as the day wore on, and the tensions through the groups along the waterfront strained as the first reports began to come. Requests from Uxbridge to military medical facility officers, naval signals advising on auxiliary personnel to be required at dockside, no specifics beyond the BBC announcement in formally turned phrases, that... "The Prime Minister has just informed the House of Commons that shortly before dawn this morning a strong Canadian Force joined by small elements of British and other United Nations troops, and escorted by ships of the Royal Navy, drove onto the French coast in the vicinity of Dieppe..."

A stir of activity followed each signal from Uxbridge, but the silence would resettle once again. The movement of fighters heading out over the channel became more frequent about midday, and once, some time after 1300 hours, a flight of Bostons appeared from out over the water escorted by six Spitfires. The port engine of the lead medium bomber was smoking and its propellor stood motionless, the bombers flying at discernibly reduced speed. They roared over the town, leaving a trace of smoke to settle and disperse in the clear, wonderfully mild air.

Shortly after 1400 hours, Spitfires tore in over Newhaven, then banked in a steep turn and streaked back out over the water, flying low. They flew almost beyond sight, then climbed and began to circle. After a time, a group of craft appeared on the horizon. The groups watched, moving closer to the docksides, as the vessels approached. Finally they could recognize two large landing craft with a motor torpedo boat as escort. The L.C.T.s moved slowly, their easily identifiable silhouettes clear against the water. As they moved closer, rounding toward the stone breakwater, their condition could be seen. And the silence began to be intruded upon by low conversation and the beginning of movement by those at the landing stages.

The landing craft were gouged and blackened, their hulls torn by shellfire. The forward ramp of one was twisted out of shape and only partially raised. Half the officers' bridge of the second had been shot away and it, too, was scored and gouged along its hull from gunfire. Fixtures hung awry into the water, and a Lewis gun could be seen, still mounted, near the bow. The patrol boat also bore signs of battle, shattered railing, a port gun emplacement that hung broken, fittings bent out of shape, its deck torn up in places. The deck of the boat was crowded with men in battle dress who did not move as they looked at the staffs and crews along the stage. The craft eased past the breakwater and their engines slacked off as they coasted in toward the stone docks. Lines were cast and retrieved and the craft tied in, coasting and scraping dully as they slid to a stop. The gunboat maneuvered alongside, its engine roaring, the waters surging beneath its stern and blue exhaust smoke trailing out.

And then they saw the men. A new silence pervaded the dock now, a silence of reality confronted, rather than one of apprehension. The sudden activity broke the stillness, and the earthly reality of war returned to the atmosphere about the waterfront. Officers and orderlies moved down to the stages, then out onto the decks of the craft. Litter bearers followed close behind. And the wounded began to be carried from the decks.

When the files of litters had cleared the ramps, the walking wounded came ashore, moving stiffly, some limping, their uniforms ragged. They came silently, their faces gray and expressionless, some being helped by orderlies, others by men in battledress who bore no wounds. Filing past a group of medical personnel, one of the men looked up slightly and nodded. He tried to smile but the expression fell apart. The procession moved slowly, filing up the short distance to the clearing station.

The unwounded moved out onto the docks, their faces equally tense, but with a certain looseness of carriage the men in pain had not shown. The dockside began to flow with the movements of men now, and officers and non-coms among the men debarking began to sort the units, calling men into groups. Sounds began to pervade the scene, and cleanly uniformed officers circulated among the groups of debarkees who were slowly led up from the docks to well guarded buildings. Some of the men spoke animatedly, seeming surprised by the sounds of their own voices. But the brittle qualities persisted, and conversation, when started, broke off sharply. Glassy-eyed, the men tried to smile.

The dead were carried off the vessels wrapped in blankets by litter bearers whose care seemed at odds with the stillness that surrounded them. Left behind, the battered naval craft retained echoes of the men they had carried, and to some, even the gunfire to which they had fallen prey.

The port became a scene of multiple activity as the day wore on. Groups of craft would approach, following the consistent pass by escort fighters. As they approached the breakwater, glowing red flares would arc across the water from some of the escort vessels, and the dockside area began to achieve a certain fragmented normalcy, a pulse of action, even if for its own sake, in place of the apprehensive waiting of the earlier hours of morning. There was constant movement of ambulances in convoy, and other vehicles, in and out of the dockside areas. Naval craft came through the breakwater to resettle the berthing facilities as the numbers of returning craft began to mount. Some of the craft arrived miraculously unscarred, carrying crews and groups of men who had been ashore, and whose condition was more that of celebration than of shock. Intelligence officers now mingled with the men across the docks, and officers of the regiments whose forces had stormed the different beaches—Royals of Canada, the Essex Scots, the R.H.L.I., Cameron Highlanders, and South Saskatchewans, Fusiliers and Royal Marines, Calgary Tankers and American Army officers. Orders rang out over loudspeaker systems, and units were marched from the docks to waiting files of lorries.

As darkness came, one arriving convoy of craft

included a landing ship with an L.C.T. in tow. As the tank craft moved to dockside, a sound of singing voices carried across the area. The men, dressed into smart formations by their noncommissioned officers, marched directly up from the craft. Their uniforms bore traces of heavy abuse, torn and shredded, some of the men only partly dressed, their boots torn and battered, their faces worn. But the sound of their voices trailed out over the dockside as they marched past the motor park to an adjacent area where lorries awaited them.

Beyond the military area, townspeople rushed to the sides of the vehicles, passing drinks and food up to the men. They stood by and called out cheerfully as the convoy moved out of the area, the lorry engines growling in low gears.

The stream of moving vehicles continued into the darkness as more vessels berthed at the docksides. The blacked-out shore area echoed to the sounds of the movement of men and equipment, the arrivals and departures of lorry convoys and ambulance trains. And the lines of covered lorries carrying the dead.

As the hours passed into the night, the confrontation with reality that had begun in the stunned silence for the units in Newhaven rose with the sense of feeling that came through from the men as they came ashore. The recognition of a feat accomplished, a battle fought and survived, an imprint of the aggressive spirit that had become, with all the pain and all the dying, the prime residual rhythm sounding through the weary, hollow-eyed, blank faced men that climbed from the broken craft that had carried them home from battle.

And sometime toward midnight, the Calpe and her sister destroyers, and the H.M.S. Locust moved through the defenses of the blacked-out naval station at Portsmouth and slid quietly to their berths.

22

Advance signals had alerted the receiving units at Portsmouth, and working silently and in darkness, teams began bringing the wounded off as soon as the destroyers had tied in. The men, suffering shock and exposure were silent, permitting themselves to be led carefully to the pierheads. Tiny lights worked by medical teams made hasty preliminary examinations and assigned the men to vehicles which carried them directly to a receiving station beyond the pierheads, or, in the case of the severely wounded, directly to ambulance trains for transport to hospitals.

In the dressing station, doctors worked quickly and efficiently, administering morphia and sulfa, while orderlies offered cigarettes and rum.

The military personnel coming off the ships who had not been among the wounded, formed up in silent columns and stepped cleanly from the decks of the ships. Coming along the pierheads, they felt the rough cobbles beneath their boots and they marched in a slow measured cadence, their uniforms barely recognizable as such, their equipment mostly left behind along the beaches of the French coast. They marched out along the stones, and their movement could be heard in the darkness.

Small groups had gathered in the yard beside the pierheads, naval personnel, men from Combined

Operations, and, standing apart, Lieutenant General A.L.G. McNaughton, Commander in Chief of the First Canadian Army, from whose ranks the raiders of Dieppe had come.

And others, too, were gathering, to begin the compiling of facts, the statistics of death, the addendum to the catalog of military records. They would, before they were finished, learn of the 3,367 casualties accounted by Canadians, 175 by the British. They would further refine the numbers to the 907 Canadians killed, 1,946 prisoners of war, the 128 British missing or prisoners of war.

They would compile the naval record of 550 casualties, including 75 killed or died of wounds and 269 missing or prisoners of war; the 67 air crew members who died, the 106 aircraft lost.

They would assess the objectives achieved, the lessons learned. They would construct the fragments of facts into a total portrait. They would ascribe lessons learned to later victories, and individual heroism would appear in dispatches, be conferred medals.

Newspaper stories would trace the fiery hells of the beaches, and emotions would rise, morale would surge for an Allied world hungry for signs of a turning point in a world three years at war.

But that would all come in the weeks and months ahead. Now, in the darkness, naval crewmen stood on the decks of destroyers and watched men march away along pierheads, then listened in darkness to the sounds of their marching until they could no longer hear them. And then they came out of the night to the tasks of refitting for a war that would continue, uninterrupted, with the next morning.

And along the beaches of Dieppe, Germans were still carrying away the Canadian wounded. And on the shore, and under the sea wall, and among the broken machines of war strewn along the gravel, the dead still lay in hundreds where they had fallen.

19 August, 1942 had come and gone, but the measure of Dieppe had only just begun.